D1421092

BIG
TROUT
FISHING

BIG TROUT FISHING

PETER COCKWILL

HAMLYN

To Geoffrey and Fiona – for their future.

Acknowledgements

With special thanks to Roy Ward of Avington Trout Fishery, Hampshire for his friendship and help in gaining the knowledge to write this book. Also for his patience over many attempts by myself and Roy Westwood to produce the photographs for this book. Thanks to Jonathon Glover of Chalk Springs Fishery, Arundel and to Ned Kelley and Graeme Watling of Duncton Mill, Sussex for their invaluable help and expert knowledge. To Malcolm Ridges of Bewl Water, Kent for his assistance and for managing such a superb fishery. To Taff Price for his company on many trips and for his unequalled advice on entomological and fly tying problems. To Bruce Vaughan of Ryobi Masterline for his help on fly lines and finally to Chris Elliot of Thrapston, Northants for his superb taxidermy skills which have made permanent momentoes of some of my best fish.

All photographs by Roy Westwood

Measurements given in this book are in imperial, but the metric units can be found by noting the imperial measurements and using the following conversion table:

Length
1 inch = 2.54 centimetres
1 foot = 30.48 centimetres
1 yard = 91.44 centimetres

Weight
1 ounce = 28.3 grams
1 pound = 0.45 kilograms

First published in 1987 by
The Hamlyn Publishing Group Ltd.,
Bridge House, London Road,
Twickenham, Middlesex.

ISBN 0 600 55168 7
Printed in Italy

CONTENTS

PREFACE

The modern trout fisherman has been weaned on the relative simplicity of throwing out a Dog Nobbler and jerking it back until the line tightens and yet another recently introduced trout ends its days in a cascade of spray at the net. So many waters demand the bare minimum of casting skills and it's really pure pot luck if the next fish that grabs hold of the Nobbler is a little better than average. The objective of this book is to help the angler who wants to broaden his or her perspectives beyond a routine of filling the freezer with stockies. There is a great deal more to the sport than just being an efficient operator of fishing tackle. Use and develop the techniques which I have evolved over the past 20 years and I promise the potential is then there to take superb specimen trout from a wide variety of waters.

Catching record fish is a feature of the search for specimen trout and in September 1986 I took a trout which I have long held the dream of achieving.

Following phone calls from friends that they had seen some large fish while fishing Avington near Winchester, Hants, I decided to take half a day's leave and fish the following morning as it was forecast to be bright and calm. My favourite conditions.

In Avington's third lake I located a really big rainbow lying under bushes. While I could have chanced dropping a nymph through the branches it was just too risky with a fish of this size so I waited for it to move out into more open water. After what seemed an age I was able to get in a clear cast. Using a leaded Hares Ear on an 8 Yorkshire Sedge I hoped the fish would respond. Immediately it saw the fly I knew I would get a take and took the chance of pulling the fly away from it twice so that when it finally took – right at the edge – setting the hook was no problem. A big trout hooked under the rod top rarely gets away from me and the 5½ lb leader put up with the fish thrashing around for some time until I could get the net under it. Only when she lay on the bank did I fully appreciate that this one was very special. A quick check on my scales made 20½ lb so it was then a case of up to the fishery office to find Roy Ward and into Winchester for formal weighing. At 20 lb 7 ozs the fish beat the existing nine year old record of 19 lb 8 ozs and as you can see from the photographs in this book was a truly superb specimen. The fish has now been set up as a permanent reminder of the day I broke the British Rainbow Trout Record.

P.C. Sept 1986

SPECIMEN TROUT OPPORTUNITIES

What makes a specimen trout such a prized quarry? Some would say it simply reflects man's most basic motives to prove himself better than his contemporaries by catching the biggest and best. Others would claim that a specimen trout represents the ultimate challenge as the oldest and most cunning inhabitant of a particular water. But rather more to the point – just what can be termed a specimen trout?

To be classed as a specimen trout we are not looking at individual or fishery records but at a fish which is an exception to the normal run for its habitat and which was perhaps unusually difficult to catch and is therefore a memorable event in a trout angler's career.

Relative sizes

To my way of thinking a 2 lb trout from an upland reservoir where stocking is either non-existent or only with fingerlings is equivalent to a four-pounder from the richer feeding of a lowland, southern reservoir where the stock fish average around 1½ lb. Then again when we look at artificially reared trout there is just as much credit in catching a fish of 5 lb from a small, lightly stocked syndicate water as there is in stalking and capturing one of the legendary giants from Avington lakes in Hampshire. The challenge is always to catch the biggest and best from any particular water at any given time of year.

Notable specimens

My best naturally grown-on brown trout is a 4 lb 2 oz fish from Cornwall's Stithians Reservoir. I have had many bigger fish but for me that Stithians specimen remains a treasured memory that rates as superior to everything that has followed. Equally important is a seemingly modest brown of 1 lb 2 oz from the old Tamar Lake in Cornwall, where I learnt my lake fly fishing. For that particular fishery a 10 oz fish used to stand out from the crowd. Then 1985 produced a grown-on rainbow from Bewl Water, Kent of 8 lb 1 oz to head a personal list of many five and six-pounders from this prolific

Left
This wild brownie was almost certainly introduced as a fingerling into Cornwall's Stithians Reservoir. This fact makes it a special prize which must be seen in perspective when making comparisons with fish from food-rich lowland waters.

Opposite
A stiff breeze on Stithians where I captured my most treasured specimen – a naturally grown-on brown trout scaling 4 lb 2 oz.

CHEETAH TROUT 9lbs 14 ozs.

water to a variety of tactics. Just as pleasing were a wild rainbow of 2 lb 6 oz from Crowdy Marsh in Cornwall, on a dry hawthorn one hot May afternoon and an old brownie of 3 lb 2 oz from a little lake near Godalming in Surrey which the National Trust used to stock annually with one hundred 6 inch browns.

The larger reservoirs offer a special challenge with their often exceptional browns. I well remember how the excitement of hooking a 6 lb 1 oz fish from Datchet's Queen Mother Reservoir was tempered by the knowledge that the then current record for the fishery stood at 6 lb 2 oz! Stafford Moor in Devon gave me my best brown on dry fly in 1977 when one of 7 lb 12 oz took a dry Daddy with absolute confidence.

The smaller stillwaters with their stocks of large, specially reared trout have always been a favourite haunt. In past years when weights fell well short of today's high averages, a rainbow of 7 lb 4 oz from Damerham, Hants, was sufficient for a prize rod from a weekly angling paper and was only 1 oz below the then water record held by Bill Sibbons. I improved my Damerham best to 8 lb 4 oz but by then Bill had put the record up to 8 lb 8 oz. Avington in Hampshire is the Mecca for those who stalk giant rainbows and a lot of effort over recent years has

given me a string of double-figure rainbows from these lovely, crystal-clear lakes. All were memorable captures but ones that stick in the mind include a beauty of 14 lb 8 oz that must have had a lot of the original steelhead in it judging by its spectacular fight. Another of 15 lb 12 oz went down the middle lake so fast that I had to get into the water to follow it round a bush. A final notable specimen stares at me from my lounge wall. At 9 lb 14 oz it's the unofficial British record cheetah trout, a real giant of its type and a particularly difficult fish to entice. Cheetahs, by the way, are a cross between rainbows and brookies.

Evolution of today's specimens

The development of stillwater trout fishing since the mid-sixties has produced a situation whereby virtually anyone with the ability to throw a fly line is in with the chance of a big fish. But, to be *consistently* successful at capturing specimen trout you cannot rely on sheer luck. Technique plus knowledge of the fish and its habits counts for everything. That's not to say that a little bit of luck now and then isn't welcome!

The huge increase in the number of waters available coupled with increased production of stock fish of all size categories has led to

a great many new converts to the world of fly fishing. Inevitably, this has brought about fundamental changes in the way fisheries are managed. Competition between waters is now quite fierce as each owner/manager tries to wrest a living wage from his business. Those Public Authorities who traditionally provided cheap, partly subsidized trout fishing for large numbers of anglers must now heed the harsh economics and apply market rates.

Hatchery techniques pioneered in Britain by the late Sam Holland at Avington resulted in selective breeding, producing fast-growing, good-looking trout which converted food efficiently. Where it was once quite acceptable to stock waters with 12 oz fish, the base individual weight must now be around 2 lb. Even this is often sneered at by many so-called anglers as just another stockie. Only 20 years ago my dream was to catch a 2 lb fish in my native Cornwall and stories of Grafham's opening days were like reading of another world.

Current situation

We have now reached the position on most small waters where a 2 lb fish is considered the norm and I know of many anglers (sportsmen) who have complained to fishery managers if their bag of fish

bows which in their third year can often approach 10 lb or even more. Not only are they used to produce the future stocks of the hatchery but they are nurtured in such a way as to ensure that when they are released into a fishery their condition is in the trophy class.

Regrettably the name jumbo rainbow has stuck and is often used to deride the capture of a very large fish – usually by those who would dearly love to have caught it!

Rearing specimen trout

Rainbow trout

Selective grading and careful feeding of a year class of trout can result in just a few having the ability to grow to specimen proportions. With care and a good water supply it's not too difficult to produce a few doubles and maybe some fish up to 14 lb within the rainbow's life span of four plus years. Most fish reach a stage beyond which they will make no further progress, will lose weight, become increasingly ugly and die. Very few hatcheries have the strain of fish or more particularly the ability to select individuals capable of exceeding 14 lb. Without a doubt Avington fishery in Hampshire excels in this speciality under the able hands and watchful eyes of Manager Roy Ward. Indeed, this famous hatchery has produced occasional fish which have exceeded 30 lb in their four-to five-year life span, but it would clearly be counter-productive to stock with such a leviathan as the British Rainbow Record would then be virtually unobtainable for all practicable purposes. It may be many years yet, or possibly never, before such exceptional fish can be considered as more than just a freak occurrence.

averaged below this figure. The larger reservoirs still rely on a basic stock fish of around 1 lb but depend on their large area and rich feeding to grow a healthy 1 lb 8 oz–2 lb fish by mid-season with a small percentage going on from year-to-year to give the likes of you and I the chance to catch a specimen.

Publicity fish

Many small waters and indeed some of our better known, well established reservoirs such as Chew and Blagdon, both near Bris-tol, stock limited numbers of the so-called 'jumbo' or brood rain-bows. These names were conjured up some ten years ago when the big stock fish boom was getting under way and it was a common sight to see in the Angling Press photographs of happy anglers posing with dark, flaccid, tailess, lumps of meat – the spent brood fish. This gave a very poor view of what can actually be achieved and I'm delighted to say that with a few exceptions such sights are a thing of the past. Many hatcheries are now capable of rearing prime conditioned rain-

Left

There's nothing quite like the Avington strain of giant rainbows. The enormous shoulders on this 14 lb fish show what selective breeding can achieve under the right conditions.

Below left

The magnificence of this Avington 16-pounder was captured just seconds after it hit the net and while it was still exhibiting its deep flush of crimson.

Brown trout

The production of our native fish, the brown trout, is a rather more complex situation. Although not too difficult to rear in the early stages they are essentially slow growers and generally demand much more attention and water space than rainbows. Certainly it is quite possible to produce double-figure browns in a hatchery environment but they really are a publicity fish as they demand the space and time which most commercial hatcheries simply cannot afford.

It's much more economical to utilize the space for the faster growing rainbow to maximize production and turnover of stock. Some of the smaller stillwaters do produce or stock a proportion of very large browns each year and indeed some are known to hold exceptional fish which continue to elude capture. Waters such as Church Hill Farm in Bucks, Leominstead in the New Forest and Rooksbury Mill, Hants all hold very large browns which are occasionally seen, very rarely hooked and almost never landed. There are ways of catching large browns in small waters but we will mostly be looking to the larger reservoirs for specimen browns. Even in these large expanses there is a further category of browns which is considered by many to be almost impossible. These are the fish well into double-figures which are seen running feeder streams in the winter months to spawn or are trapped in gill netting operations to remove unwanted pike. I believe that they are almost entirely night feeders who remain virtually torpid during daylight hours.

Consider the evidence. To grow so big they must feed heavily and to do so in daylight and avoid capture would demand a cautious intelligence they simply cannot possess. They almost certainly feed on small coarse fish and the actual period of feeding activity is relatively short. I doubt that fly fishing in the accepted sense of the sport will ever be able to satisfactorily crop these fish. On the very rare occasion that one is caught it usually happens on a very stormy day or at dusk before convention and regulations dictate that anglers must leave the water. Either that or they are sometimes contacted at great depth where to all intents and purposes it is permanently dark. The passage of large, trolled lures possibly creates sufficient disturbance to arouse the curiosity of one of these predators much as the use of trolled spoons and such like will pick them up on the large Scottish and Irish waters.

Less common species

Clearly there are many opportunities to search for and catch specimen rainbows and browns but what of the other types of trout found in this country?

The American brook trout

This species has been with us for many years and is currently headed by one of 5 lb 13½ oz taken in 1981 by Alan Pearson at Avington. In their native land they grow much larger but it seems that conditions just are not right over here for them to achieve their full potential.

It is said that the strain is becoming weak and that fresh stock is needed to be imported but the cost of such shipment is beyond the resources of most hatcheries for a fish which figures very low in total production. There are good brookies to be found in some small waters from time to time and just occasionally a specimen crops up from one of the more northern reservoirs where it has succeeded in growing on. Currently I would rate any brookie of 3 lb and over as a specimen even if hatchery reared.

The cheetah (brook × rainbow) and tiger (brook × brown)

These are the other realistic specimen trout options. Named because of their markings, these interesting hybrids were once hailed as the saviour of winter fishing in that they are sterile and therefore remain in condition throughout the year. Also it was thought that their growth rates would be correspondingly phenomenal. Sadly both options proved incorrect. First, orders for the hybrids were slow to arrive and when you bear in mind that a hatchery must plan its stock for three years ahead, it's no good having ponds full of fish that no one wants.

Second, although initial growth rates were good the fish just did not progress much beyond 5 lb in either group and only the odd individuals made much more. Tigers achieved a ceiling weight of around 7 lb and the cheetah best was 9 lb 14 oz. Unless these hybrids again become popular they are of little concern to current hunters of specimen trout.

Triploid

One final trout worth mentioning is the triploid. Essentially a sterile, female rainbow, it again exhibits excellent initial growth rates and

can be a remarkably handsome fish. Double-figure specimens are a distinct possibility on some waters and will inevitably be hatchery reared fish. Although their behaviour and habits are identical to large rainbows it is possible to distinguish them in clear water fisheries by their brighter, less spotted body.

Fighting qualities

Much has been said about large hatchery reared fish being a pushover in terms of fighting potential. Certainly this was, and still is, true of spent brood fish with their lumpy, tailless bodies but the modern carefully reared, fully finned rainbow is a much different proposition. I know that some simply seem to give up when hooked but this is just as true of fish in the 1–2 lb range – they are all individuals. Many specimen trout are lost simply because of panic by the angler or maybe inexperience – not because of the fish's fighting ability and later on I will cover tactics to overcome these problems. If I had to choose then I believe that pound-for-pound a grown-on reservoir fish fights better than a specimen of equivalent proportions from a small stillwater. But of course they are being tackled in very different environments. The majority of large trout will give a very good account of themselves if hooked at a range of at least ten yards on tackle which is not over powerful.

Easy to catch hatchery specimens?

It's a commonly held belief that large, hatchery-reared fish when released into small waters are simple to catch. If that's true then why do so many people fish these waters in the hope of catching one and yet it's only a small percentage of anglers who hook the majority of the specimens? Watching

Right
A real beauty of a brownie from the stews at Chalk Springs fishery in Sussex. Our native species is a slow developer and costly to rear.

Below
Dawn in the New Forest and time to reflect on just how big the brownies might have become in Leominstead's deep, cool waters. It is one of several fisheries where very large browns are occasionally seen.

such an angler at work will often give the impression that indeed it is rather easy but then the same applies to watching an expert in any subject. Providing you can handle a fly rod reasonably competently you should be in with an excellent chance of catching a real specimen.

Where to find specimen trout

In essence there are now a great many waters offering today's trout fly fisher the opportunity to catch a specimen, be it a wild brown of 2 lb from a moorland reservoir or a double-figure fish from a small stillwater. All are relative to their own particular environment and size alone is not the criteria in deciding the worth of a specimen. However, in relative terms how do you go about deciding where to fish and for what size of trout? The best guide must be the weekly or monthly returns of the various fisheries published in the Angling Press. From these figures it is possible to work out the potential of a particular water. Does it produce specimen trout consistently or are they very few and far between? Some reservoirs and a great many small waters produce the occasional really large trout in relation to their normal stock but these are usually what are known as 'publicity fish'. Sometimes these are just old brood stock which would not survive another summer and are introduced early in the season but more often they are just individual specimens bought in with the normal consignment of fish with the sole intention of getting the fishery some free

publicity and so drawing in more anglers.

With advertising costs as they are, a picture in the Angling Press has to be well worth the investment in a couple of big trout. However, in most instances the capture of such fish is down to pure chance especially if the lake is large or has coloured water. It could be my fly it takes or that of a complete beginner. Where there's just one good fish among hundreds of average size then hunting such specimens is just not a realistic pursuit.

The waters to visit are those whose reputation is so well established that they do not need to advertise or quote returns and those whose returns show they consistently stock a good proportion of large trout and where there is clearly a chance on any visit of finding a big fish feeding. These are generally the smaller waters

of ten acres or less and can be grouped under the broad classifications of coloured and clear water – each requiring different tactics (see page 57).

The larger waters up to reservoirs of many hundreds of acres can frequently offer grown-on specimens, sometimes only in the first few weeks of the season but more often at intervals throughout the year building to a peak in the months of September and October.

These then are the various types of water where specimen trout can be found. I will mention current fisheries capable of producing specimens but be alert to changes in ownership or style of management which can lead to different characteristics in stock density, turnover and average size with the consequent increase or decrease in the chance of coming across our quarry – the specimen trout.

A sterile Tiger from Nythe Lakes in Hampshire. This hybrid failed to make a great impact on the angler and has become a rarity these days.

TACKLE

There is now an immense choice of tackle on the market and for a relative beginner it can be terribly confusing when trying to select, say, a suitable rod for a particular water or style of fishing. With rods made of cane, glass, carbon, and boron – all with particular characteristics and merits – it can often come down simply to a matter of how much you can afford.

I most certainly do not advocate buying the most expensive equipment available and neither should it be too powerful. Some years ago when hatchery-reared fish were approaching 20 lb it was stated by several eminent anglers that conventional fly rods simply would not be capable of handling such large fish. Frankly, that is nonsense. I have been saying for several years that we are all using gear which is much too powerful for the size of fish being caught. And I conclusively proved my case in 1985 when I spent three weeks in Oregon, USA, fly fishing the wild rivers for steelhead (migrating rainbows) and salmon. All I used were 7/8 rated carbon or glass rods around 9 ft 6 in in length mated to reels with at least 150 yards of backing and powerful braking systems. With leaders of 12 lb breaking strain I had steelhead up to 10 lb which performed spectacularly. But the power of the rod was never in doubt. Fly fishing for Chinook or King Salmon in powerful water full of rocks and timber would, I was sure, be courting disaster on that sort of tackle but even these powerful fish showed that our trout rods have plenty of power in them. It's certainly one hell of a battle but it won't be the rod that goes. Watching Jim Teeny, who is the undoubted Oregon expert, I frequently saw his normal graphite rods in an almost full hoop while he put on maximum pressure. I caught a great many Chinook averaging about 20 lb and some up to 30 lb and never had any worries about my rods.

Contrasting requirements

For most small water fishing the basic tackle set up needs to be a medium weight outfit – that is in terms of line loading and an AFTM 7 or thereabouts is quite adequate. Accuracy and delicacy of approach is the principal requirement of the tackle for small waters. The larger lakes and reservoirs generally demand the use of tackle capable of casting considerable distances, often in strong winds, and this usually means a more powerful rod matched to a heavier line up to AFTM 9. It is possible to settle for an 8-rated outfit to cover maybe 60–70 percent of the joint requirements of both types of water but I would personally prefer to have a much greater choice of equipment available.

Equipment for small waters

Rods

What will be the principal requirements of a rod for tackling specimen trout on small waters? Certainly it will not need to cast a long way and neither will it need to be particularly long for line control. Conversely, a very short rod would be a nuisance when fishing among high reeds. This leads to the choice of something in the 9 ft to 9 ft 6 in range and I very much favour what is called a through-action rod. This is where the rod bends progressively throughout its length as opposed to a tip-actioned rod which essentially only really bends in the top half. These latter rods are great for distance casting where high line speed and tight loop control are so necessary but they don't give me a feeling of confidence when it's necessary to put a lot of pressure on a big fish.

The current vogue is for powerful tip-actioned rods – often termed Nobbler outfits – and even fitted with extension butts to fight the fish. Just who are we trying to kid? There isn't a fish in this country that needs such gimmicks, unless of course an angler has a particularly weak wrist and needs to support the rod under the forearm. With my conventional through action rods and those Oregon salmon I could put on plenty of pressure, even to the extent of feeling the handle corks opening up.

If you really need to put on some extra pressure to fight a big fish then hold the line to the handle with the fingers of the right hand – assuming you play a fish right handed – and lift the rod about a foot up from the handle with the left hand. This technique puts on a lot of extra pressure and is very useful for holding a big fish steady when at close range. I think that for most small water tactics a rod rated for a 7 or 8 weight line will cope with anything that swims in this country.

On occasions when I have had big fish on 5/6 rated rods in difficult swims, full of snags or weed, then I don't feel happy with the sideways waggle of such a rod when under a lot of pressure with a fish on a short line. As for materials, there isn't much to choose between either cane, glass, carbon or boron, providing that the

Right
*Not recommended – but proof
that today's graphite rods are
built to absorb punishment!*
Centre
*The through-action rod (top) is
superior for playing big fish
while the tip model performs
best for distance casting.*
Bottom
*Why bother with an extension
butt unless you've got a weak
wrist.*

action is correct. Cane rods are generally heavier than anything else and carbon or boron blanks have a very slim appearance but for the sort of work the outfit is expected to do then it really doesn't matter a great deal. Glass is the cheapest option although some of the less expensive carbon rods have quite a pleasant through action for this style of fishing. I personally prefer carbon because of its extreme lightness and also its ability to recover its original mode quickly after being flexed. I find that this suits my way of casting better than glass rods as with small leaded nymphs I need to be quick and extremely accurate.

For many years I have used a 7/8 Hardy graphite 9¼ ft nymph-style rod and have only recently replaced it because the ferrule was getting so slack. I'm now using a rod made up from a Lamiglass LHS blank rated AFTM 8 and 9 ft 6 in long. These blanks have a delightful through action but are very strong and give the close accurate line control that I need.

Line guides

I fix the butt ring only 13 inches up from the handle instead of the more normal 22 to 24 inches so I don't have to grab such a large loop of line between reel and butt ring after casting or when retrieving. As long as the tip and butt rings are lined with a hard-wearing material I'm not too bothered about the rest of the intermediates.

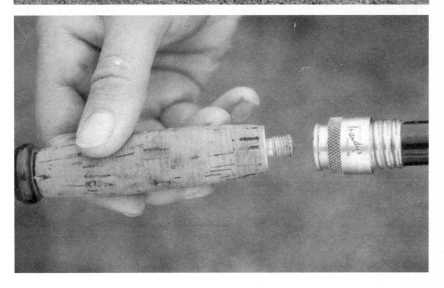

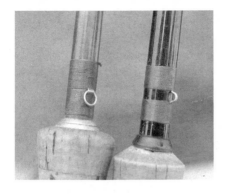

Above and right
Keeper rings are handy but I prefer to carry my rod set up so that the leader/fly line junction is outside the rod top.

Opposite top
Who says conventional fly tackle can't cope with the biggest trout? This 30 lb Chinook was captured among rocks and floating timber in Oregon using nothing more powerful than a slim carbon rod built to aerialize a No. 7 line.

Opposite bottom
The Lamiglass blank cushions a plunging rainbow on a short line. **Inset** *I made up this rod from blanks purchased in the States.*

Right
Snake, bridge and lined single leg rings. Take your pick.

I went through a period of equipping all my rods with Fuji rings throughout. But for practical fishing purposes I can't see how the minor advantage of less friction at the line-to-ring contact points can make a significant difference in casting performance for the small water angler. Intermediate guides can be snake, bridge, or single leg type. Take your choice – I use snake because they are light, flexible and cheap.

Fine detail on rods

Handle shape isn't too important but it must be thick enough to grip comfortably. A thin handle causes

Fly line protrudes through tip ring ready for immediate action

Leader looped around reel and back up rod to secure fly on ring

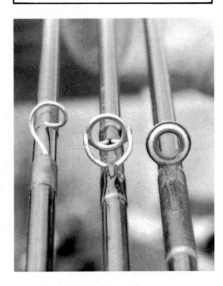

your grip to be too tight and is very tiring as the muscles of the hand are unnaturally strained. That kind of unnecessary tension can badly affect concentration. Modern carbon blanks are now so thin that normal handles look a bit

out of place on them. So beware of rods which may perhaps look better proportioned but possibly at the expense of handle thickness.

Matt varnish or a quick rub down with very fine wet-and-dry glasspaper will reduce the chances of the sun glinting off the rod and possibly scaring a fish. And a screw reel grip is a must. They are now available in extremely lightweight materials and do keep the reel secure. There's nothing worse than a reel falling off when a big fish is on.

One final point is whether to fit a keeper ring. It's true they are handy but I carry my rod set up so that the leader/fly line junction is outside the rod top and it's easy to quickly unhook the fly for immediate action.

Reels

The chief function of a reel on small waters is to act as storage for the line. Providing it has an exposed rim and a sound check mechanism then it need only be large enough to hold maybe 30 yards of backing and fly line. When hunting very large fish I'd definitely become extremely worried if one ever gained the whole fly line from me in battle! If you can afford it then there are some quite lovely reels available at prices up to £60 or £70. They're superb pieces of engineering but a £10 Leeda Rimfly will do the same job.

Nowadays I use Hardy Marquis No. 7 or 8 models because I doubt that I will ever wear them out and they adequately perform all the tasks I require from them on small waters. I'm not at all keen on automatic reels because of their extra weight and often unpredictable drag. And neither can I see any need for geared rates of retrieve.

Loading the reel so that the line comes to within ¼ inch of the full spool will give a perfectly adequate retrieve rate for all normal purposes. The single most important thing is to ensure at all times

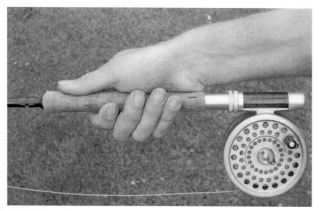

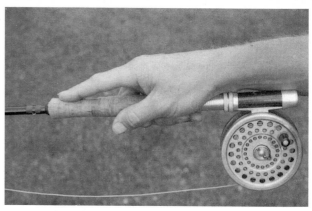

Above, left and right
Thumb on top for winding up to a long cast (left) or forefinger where accuracy is the priority.

Below
Hardy Marquis reels – built to last.

Below
Screw reel grip (top) and traditional sliding sleeve on corks. There's only one choice.

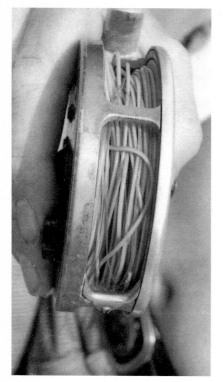

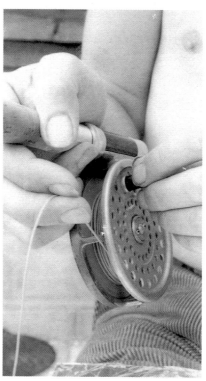

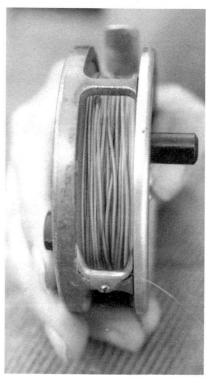

Loose coils of line are just asking for trouble.

Make a habit of rewinding tightly in even layers.

Correctly loaded reel that will feed line smoothly.

that the line is evenly and tightly wound on the reel. Loose coils are just asking for trouble when a large fish suddenly wants line or indeed at the start of a day when the first pull on the end of the leader to thread it through the rings results in the nylon biting down into the loose coils and jamming the reel.

Lines

Fly lines are produced in a seemingly endless variety of weights, profiles, finishes and colours as well as all these variables in floating, sink tips or full sinkers from intermediates to lead cores. Fortunately for small water fishing there is no need to make life too complicated.

Let me first of all describe the basic line profiles. The simplest is a level line, rarely used nowadays unless as backing in its lightest weight to shooting heads. Probably the most popular line is the double taper which is thickest in the middle and runs with a continuous taper to each end. The weight forward profile is sometimes exaggerated into the long

belly, both of which have the initial short taper leading into a heavy section backed up by finer level line. The final variety is the shooting head which is roughly a half line similar to the main part of a weight forward and often comes ready joined to a running line of either braided or flat monofilament. There are other variations on these profiles but in essence a double taper is the line to use where delicacy and accuracy are the paramount requirements. Where pure distance or speed of reaction in putting out a fly are the main functions then forward tapers or shooting heads come into their own.

Colour

There has been a great deal of controversy in recent years about the effect of white lines. Although I have used all colours I can't say that any one particular shade scares fish more than another. Certainly this applies only to floating lines which it must be remembered are seen from below by the fish and in all probability appear simply as a dark line whatever their colour. Without doubt a line

will frighten fish, particularly those near the surface in very clear water, but under the same circumstances and light conditions I truly consider that any colour of line would evoke the same reaction. In other words it's the presence of the line or the way it is being used rather than its colour which spooks the fish.

Having said this in relation to floating lines, I will be quite adamant and declare that sinking lines should match the environment or appear as unobtrusive as possible. This basically means using greens and browns. Perhaps one day an enterprising manufacturer will come up with a mottled line coating, then we really would be able to blend into the surroundings.

Lines for small water fishing

The most useful line for small water fishing is a double taper and it will need to be either a 6 or 7 weight to match the rod (page 20). As for its colour, then bear in mind that it's you that needs to see the line so as to detect takes – unless you are stalking individuals by sight. Therefore, use whatever colour you think will be best.

I personally prefer the softer pastel shades such as sand or peach rather than say bright yellow or orange and it's far more important that the line remains supple so that casting performance will be at its best.

By all means make regular use of plasticizing agents on your lines but as soon as they start to crack up or go out in coils then it's time to replace them.

The other lines you will need for the small water tactics I will be describing are weight forward sevens in an intermediate and medium sinking rate. A Wet Cell I or II will be ideal for the latter and that's the fastest sinking outfit you should need for small waters.

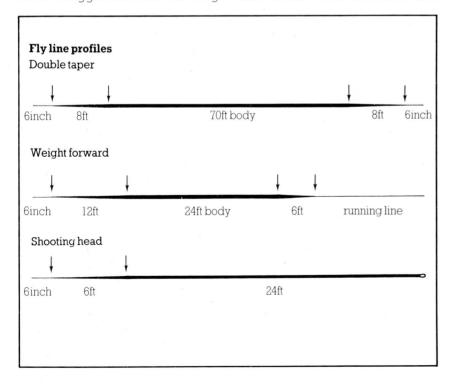

Fly line profiles
Double taper

6inch   8ft   70ft body   8ft   6inch

Weight forward

6inch   12ft   24ft body   6ft   running line

Shooting head

6inch   6ft   24ft

Fly lines are manufactured in all colours of the rainbow – and a good many more besides! Ryobi Masterline have marketed an amazing 98 different shades in recent years and here is a small selection of lines from their current range. From right: apple green, white, chestnut brown, pale yellow, mint green, hot orange, sand brown, peach, dapple grey, sand and green.

Leaders

In its simplest form a leader can just be a length of monofilament joined to the fly line but there is now such a range available that it's fast becoming a specialized subject.

There are continuous tapers in solid or braided nylon, special finishes for either floating or sinking varieties and complex mixes of diameters to achieve particular performance characteristics.

The simplest form of leader is a single length of nylon. This does not perform very well in terms of presentation but it is satisfactory while learning to cast when knots and tangles soon ruin a leader. However, it's much better to make up a taper by knotting together different diameters. A straightforward stepped leader will cast well and its length can be varied by altering the tippet length. It has

the disadvantages of a number of knots to induce line-wake and means more potential weak areas when under strain. Also it's easier to hook up when casting and little bits of weed snag more often.

A substantial improvement is to use a purpose-made continuous taper leader and attach new tippets as required. These ready-made leaders are available in a wide variety of butt and tip diameters, lengths from 7 ft to 18 ft, different colours and even with special finishes to make them either float or sink. Indeed some are also treated to eliminate glare from the nylon surface. This type has formed the basis of my small water leader design for many years. I use a 'salmon' size tapering down to a 7 lb point. I cut off the butt loop and the first 18 in of heavy taper, as this tends to coil up too easily. I then attach it to the fly line with a needle knot and finally put

on a 5 or 6 lb tippet to give an overall leader length of about 10 feet.

Braided leaders

These are an impressive development in leader design with their main virtues being extreme suppleness with no 'memory' to retain coils and the ability to turn over a leader quite beautifully and therefore aid the presentation of the fly.

The continuous taper models perform particularly well and the method of attachment to the fly line with a short length of silicone tube appears at first sight to be very suspect but it most certainly works. I'm not keen on the method of attaching tippets to braided leaders but for casting into or across a wind I don't think they can be bettered. It's very common to see people put out a reasonable line into a wind, or for that matter with a wind, but fail to achieve any form of leader turnover such that the fly lands closer to the angler than the end of the fly line. More

Leaders

Basic stepped leader

	6lb		8lb	12lb	20lb	Fly line
	60 inch		24inch	18inch	18inch	

Tapered leader and tippet

6lb		Continuous taper		Fly line
2ft-12ft		9ft		

Tapered braided leader and tippet

6lb		Continuous taper braid		Fly line
2ft-12ft				Tubing connector

Left
Continuous taper nylon leaders –
one with a non-flash finish.

Middle
Revolution tapered leader made
of twisted mono for use with dry
flies. It's considered that this
type of leader is more capable
of absorbing smash takes when
using a light point.

Below left
Tapered, braided leader from
the Ryobi Masterline sinker
series. The suppleness of this
material helps achieve precise
presentation of the fly.

Below
**Attaching a Revolution Tapered
Braided Leader to a fly line**
1 Push end of fly line into open
braid at butt end of leader and
thread it through for about an
inch.
2 Cut off a length of the plastic
tubing, about $\frac{3}{4}$ inch, and thread
it on to the other end of leader.
3 Run tubing all the way along to
where fly line enters braided
monofil and ease it over the con-
nection so that the end of the
braid is midway under the tube.

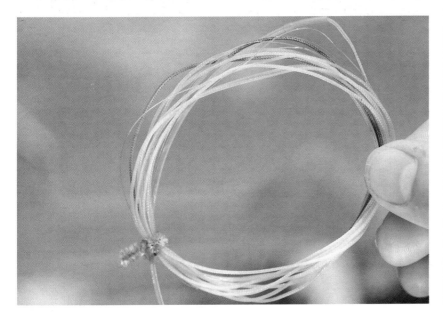

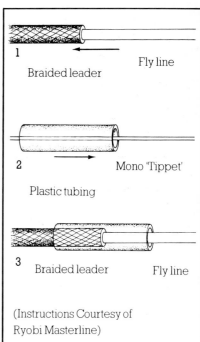

1   Braided leader   Fly line

2   Mono 'Tippet'

Plastic tubing

3   Braided leader   Fly line

(Instructions Courtesy of
Ryobi Masterline)

Left
Spools of nylon rattle in the tackle bag for months on end but they should be regularly tested for signs of deterioration

Below and opposite
Forget about triangular landing nets with floppy cord at the leading edge – they won't push through weed. This Gye salmon net has a solid rim and sliding shaft with quick-release strap for one-handed operation.

care with casting technique, particularly the need to make a tight loop on the back cast, will usually improve this fault as will pulling back sharply on the fly line at the moment of delivery, but the addition of a braided leader will help more than anything else to achieve a good presentation.

I first seriously used braided leaders in the 1985 French Open Fly Fishing Championships on a lake at Dreux – south of Paris. Big fish were not the quarry as the event was scored on total length but as the match was fished in short sessions at a variety of peg positions it was vital to achieve good presentation, particularly when putting out into a stiff wind and I picked up enough fish from almost every peg to come second overall.

Since then I have been sold on them for effective presentation in windy conditions. Braided leaders come in floating or sinking versions and some can even be treated with special compounds to make them either float or sink as required. I will go into leader lengths in more detail when describing specific tactics in chapters 4 and 5.

Powergum

This is again a relatively recent innovation and involves knotting a short length of an elastic material into the leader to absorb shocks

and reduce breakages. It may well be useful to those who fish very fine points but I am only concerned with catching specimen trout and don't ever go below a 4 lb tippet. If you are getting broken then I don't think Powergum will help. There is either a basic fault in the handling of large fish or the tackle set-up is completely out of balance. I have seen a lot of specimens lost by people using leaders of adequate strength but mated to lines and rods far too heavy, making an outfit which is unbalanced and has no sense of feel to it.

Nylon colour

Whatever type of leader you decide to use, the tippet length will be of nylon and as this is the section of line a fish is most likely to see because it's attached to the fly then it pays to put a bit of thought into it. Where the water is clear, be it small lake or reservoir, then I much prefer nylon that is either a smoke or tan colour. My current favourite brand is Racine Tortue which is a pleasant neutral colour and quite supple.

Landing nets

Small water fishing usually entails a degree of mobility and therefore a landing net needs to be capable of being easily carried preferably by being attached in some way to the angler. I used to carry around a good sized triangular net on a long handle but was forever leaving it lying on the bank a long way from where I hooked a fish. Now it is possible to lift out by hand trout of several pounds in weight and I have successfully done this with fish up to 8 lb by gripping them across the back just behind the head. But it's a risky game. Far better to be properly equipped with a good net. Specimens are not going to be hooked every day and it would be a real shame to lose one because of a bungled landing job.

In a similar vein it is sometimes possible to beach a big trout by drawing it into shallow water so that it lies on its side with the head partially out. Keeping a tight line you then grip the fish by the gills and lift it out. Sounds easy but if the fish struggles the moment you get hold of it then believe me it's not easy to hold on to several pounds of thrashing trout. Whatever you try with your own fish don't ever offer to land one by hand for a friend. That really is courting disaster and is a sure way to end a friendship if it all goes wrong. Similarly, unless you can really absolutely trust them don't let anyone else net your own fish. Do it yourself then there is only one person to blame.

For all my needs on small stillwaters I am very happy with the type of net which slides on a square shaft and can be carried slung on the back with a quick release strap arrangement. Farlow's 'Gye' salmon net in its 20 in diameter size will cope with

the biggest trout you are ever likely to hook in this country. It's very strong, easy to use and has a solid rim making it possible to push into weed to net a fish that has become stuck fast. There is a smaller 'sea trout' version which is ideal for waters where you are not going to come across fish over 10 lb.

Fly boxes

The range of flies I use on small waters is easily carried in two small boxes or wallets. One is for the leaded bugs used on clear waters and the other is reserved for the generally larger flies fished on coloured waters and which will also hold a few dry flies. Simple 6 inch by 4 inch plastic boxes lined with ethafoam have served me well for many years and are readily available in tackle shops. I know that many people, myself included, consider that flies in felt-paged wallets quickly become squashed and as they are not so easy to dry out hooks can soon go rusty. There is nothing worse than at last hooking a specimen trout only to have the hook break and so you should eliminate the possibility of rust getting hold. A pin or needle is useful to clear varnish from hook eyes or to tie on new leaders if required. The type with large coloured heads are most easily spotted.

All the previously mentioned items can be regarded as the main requirements of a small water angler's kit but the extras can then amount to a substantial bulk unless you are prepared to do as I suggest and travel light.

Clothing

Unless it's actually raining, when a Barbour type coat is essential, I only ever wear a waistcoat on top of either a jumper or shirt. Incidentally, don't make the common mistake of wearing the latest smart

Above

A wide-brimmed, Western-style hat and good-quality Polaroids with amber lenses give me a real edge when fish-spotting in clear waters. I often locate trout that many anglers have walked straight past.

Opposite

My waistcoat with the pockets turned out to show what I carry during a typical day's stalking on a small water.

waistcoat over a white shirt. Keep all your clothes in browns and greens or mottled patterning. Walking boots or wellingtons are fine but make sure they are comfortable. On some small waters you may well walk several miles in a day's fishing.

Hat and Polaroids

My leather western-style hat is rather battered and is often un-

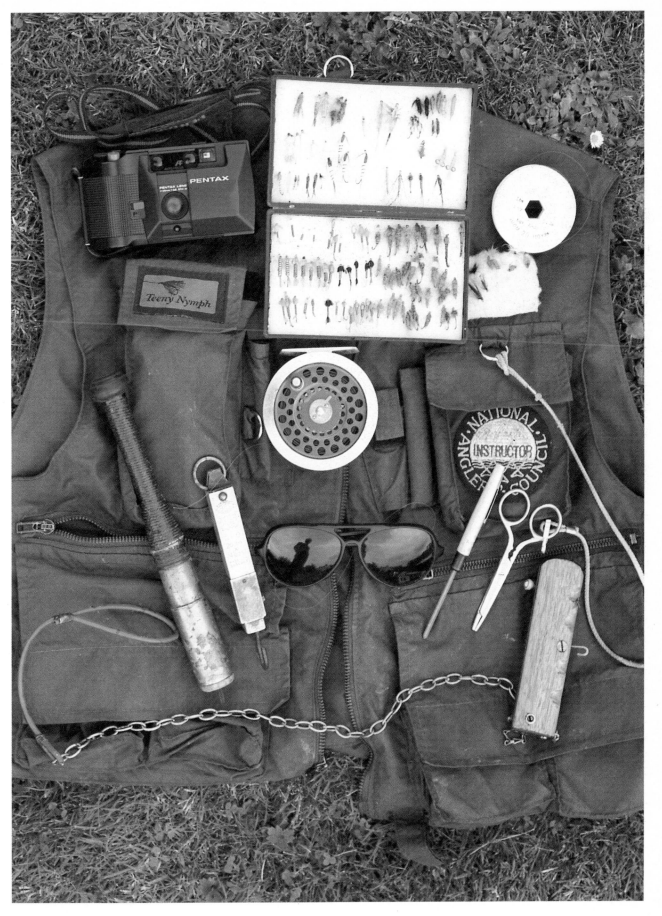

kindly described as a cowpat but it makes all the difference when looking into water. Anything with a brim or peak will suffice but again don't wear something white. The shade cast over your eyes will make the water surface non-existent when coupled with good Polaroids. Do buy the best – I used to purchase cheap pairs and replaced them every few months. But after I bought my first pair of Optics I realized why I had previously suffered bad headaches after two or three hours of intensive water watching. Cheap polarizing sunglasses are not optically perfect and will put additional strain on the eyes. There is quite a bit of controversy about lens colour but for me amber tint is the most comfortable on small waters. I like grey the best on reservoirs and only use yellow for looking into white water on rivers. My eyesight is by no means excellent but I have always had the ability to look into water and spot fish and will try to explain further in the chapter on small water tactics.

Pocket essentials

Empty out my waistcoat pockets and you'll find the following:
● A stout pair of blunt-ended scissors on a length of string or attached to one of these neat little retractable springs.
● Small spools of spare tippet material in 4, 5 and 6 lb breaking strain and a good hook-sharpening device. I like the Eze-lap which clips in like a pen.
● Small pot of fly floatant and a paste of Fullers Earth with washing-up liquid to degrease leaders go in the same pocket as my priest, stringer and scales.

Priests

There are some beautifully made priests available but make sure that it is at least 10 in long and weighs about 6–8 oz.

Once your big trout is on the bank there is no virtue in pussy footing about with a lightweight priest. Kill the fish quickly and cleanly with a single blow. My father made up mine from the end of an old Hoover nozzle which he filled with lead. It's a sure end for any trout I catch.

Stringer

This is easy to carry and ensures that the fish will remain in good condition. It can be anything from a bit of string to a purpose-made job like mine. Again produced by my father from an idea of mine, it makes it easy to carry a brace of doubles back to the car. I learnt the hard way how difficult it is to carry big trout on just a length of cord after my first four-fish 40 lb limit from Avington.

Scales

Do carry a small set of scales. Although most fisheries have a set they are frequently somewhat generous in their weighings and by testing mine regularly I can say quite truthfully exactly what each of my fish weighs.

Extras

I like to have a bottle of midge repellant – Jungle Formula works for me but body odours do vary in their attractiveness to flies so try out a few to find the repellant that suits you. There must be something extra tasty about me because the months of June and July are a real pain from the attentions of the dreaded 'cleg' – commonly and incorrectly called a horse fly.

Finally, there are two extra items which are quite useful in tracking down specimen trout. Where it's usual to fish just one or two spots during a day you may well find a lightweight three-legged stool to be very useful. I can still put out a whole WF8 from a seated position so it's a very comfortable way to fish. A plastic refuse bag occupies no space at all

and is useful to keep the rain off your tackle bag and can be used to take the catch back home.

That then is all the gear you need for fishing small waters when playing the stalking game. It makes for a very light comfortable approach.

Additional tackle for coloured waters

On the fisheries where you either cannot see into the water or where the lake is reasonably large and perimeter stalking tactics don't work, then you will commonly need to carry possibly two rods with extra reel spools loaded with alternative lines. That's when it pays to put everything into a small satchel.

Reservoir tackle: bank and boat

Fishing the larger waters means coping with much more exposed weather conditions, the general need to cast considerably farther and the rather more specialized requirements of boat fishing. Progressing on from the tackle used for small water fishing, I am more than confident of the power of the rods to deal with the size of fish expected and in many instances the rods used on small waters will be quite adequate for the larger reservoirs. The principal difference is that the fish are usually fought at much longer range and frequently run for considerable distances under circumstances where it is quite impossible to follow them. This inevitably means that reels must carry larger quantities of backing. However, let's first discuss rods.

Three rods and rather more choice of flies for a day's reservoir fishing at Bewl Water.

Left
A substantial lead core rod with my Lamiglass model alongside for comparison. There's not a great deal of sensation fighting a fish on such heavy gear.

Opposite
A large spool on the Carbon Lineshooter reduces coiling in the backing.

the more the tip-action rod comes into its own.

While nothing like as pleasant when bending into a good fish, it is well worth using for its ability to maintain a much narrower loop in the air when casting. A narrow loop affords very little air resistance and therefore the energy put into the line by the casting action is fully utilized instead of being lost when throwing a large loop which will dissipate much of its latent energy in pushing the line through the air in a wide arc. But I'm often more than happy to sacrifice say five yards of distance so that I can use a softer rod and maintain a better feel for my fishing. Distance work therefore from bank or boat requires an 8/9 outfit basically tip-actioned and something on the lines of a Hardy Farnborough will adequately cope.

Lead core rods I have fished with lead core lines and caught good trout on them and accept there are circumstances when they'll produce exceptional specimens. But I like to experience a good fight from my fish and feel this is not possible when the hooked trout has to pull around a great length of lead core line. However, in the pure sense of catching specimens, lead core tactics have their use and if you want to do this style of fishing you will need a specialized rod. Trying to throw lead lines on normal reservoir tackle is asking for premature fail-

Rods

For nymph and dry fly work a 6/7 rated rod again in soft action admirably suits my tactics but for reservoirs I much prefer some extra length and currently use a 10 ft 6 in Bruce and Walker Multitrout. This extra length allows for good control of the fly when nearing the end of a retrieve and also permits easy line lift off to cover a rising fish quickly. Rods for distance casting both from bank and boat need to be rated 8/9 so that they have some beef to cope with wind and

need to be at least 9 ft in length and preferably of carbon. This material, or indeed boron, offers the least wind resistance because of its fine diameter and over a long day coping with strong winds can make a tremendous difference to angler fatigue.

Through-action rods Having said that through-action rods are much more preferable for fighting specimen trout, we are now into the realms of needing to cast greater distances and therefore

tackling a whole day of long-distance casting. Because of the need to carry a larger variety of lines it's usually necessary to load a variety of reels simply because it would be too costly to standardize. I use several different makes and style of reel which are all perfectly satisfactory providing they carry the amount of line I recommend. But remember the reel is still essentially only for carrying line. I have often taken the reel off the rod when reservoir fishing and popped it in a coat pocket just so that I don't have to wave its weight around when casting. Apart from a lead core outfit, you will need to carry the following lines for the methods I use to catch grown-on reservoir specimens.

Lines

I carry a 6 or 7 double taper floater plus a weight forward 8 or 9 in both intermediate and Wet Cell II sinking rates. Shooting heads to achieve extra distance are a must and a fast-sinking Hi Speed Hi D with a full floater both in weight 9 will give a good range of lines to cope with most conditions. You can manage by using spare spools and say just having three main reels with a spare spool for each, one taking a lead core. I like two rods set up when bank fishing and three when out in a boat as it's a positive nuisance having to change lines to suit conditions which on some days can alter every half hour.

Competition style

There is another style of fly fishing currently very fashionable and popular which is rapidly evolving its own specialized tackle requirements. This is competition fishing loosely based on traditional loch-style tactics. I consider it to be an absolute non-starter in terms of attracting specimens, although of course exceptions will always turn up and Bob Draper's 7 lb Grafham brown was just such a notable fish.

ure of the rod. I use an 11 ft 6 in rod made up from a blank supplied by Tom Saville of Nottingham. Mated to a 450 grain shooting head I can put out a measured 53 yards on grass and can maintain 40 plus yards for quite a long time before my elbow finally gives out.

Reels

Reels need to be capable of holding a full WF 8 or 9 line and at least 70 yards, or preferably 100 yards, of backing. These large reservoir trout can and do run a long way. I am very fond of the Carbon Lineshooter by Advanced Angling Limited even though I was foolish enough to use it on American Chinook and have the neoprene braking rings melt under the stress of very fast 100-yard downstream runs. My waistcoat still carries the marks made by the fast revolving spool rim as I tried to slow it even more than the drag. This reel has a large spool diameter so reducing coiling of the backing and is also extremely light which is a big plus factor when

Essentially it's a system of catching large numbers of very recently introduced small fish as quickly as possible and as such is not in contention for our principal aim of removing the comparatively few large fish in each reservoir. My methods are all about consistently taking specimens and a little example will demonstrate how some tactics just don't apply. For my first couple of seasons on Bewl Water in Kent my regular boat partner fished just one basic style – lure stripping – and because it's very difficult to mix styles in the same boat I had to follow suit. True, we caught a great many fish and rarely failed to come in with double limits. But overwintered fish were extremely rare. They were being caught purely by chance! It wasn't until I persuaded my partner to try out some of my tactics that we started to boat some pretty impressive specimens. His first really good one of 6½ lb in 1982 was, I believe, the third best rainbow of the season. It's the methods and not necessarily the tackle or flies which will consistently catch specimen trout.

Well-balanced tackle is clearly an advantage for achieving a level of performance which will then leave plenty of scope for thought when applying tactics to take fish which have often been in a reservoir for several years and seen an awful lot of flies in that time.

Additional tackle for reservoir bank fishing

Leaders
These are much as before except that they will be substantially longer, often to 20 feet or more.

Fly boxes
The variety of flies used is generally much larger than for small waters and fly boxes therefore need to be more numerous or much larger. The wooden type is very popular and I have used two for many years. I carry around a thousand flies for any reservoir trip and that lot takes up a fair bit of space.

Satchel
A roomy waterproof satchel will also serve to carry some food and drink as it's quite likely that you will walk a considerable distance from your car. There is a lot of pleasure in just relaxing over a snack when out in the country and it's well worth making a conscious effort to stop for a while and take a good look around at what is going on.

Clothing
Clothes for bank fishing need to be fully waterproof as there is rarely much shelter available. Remember that even in high summer it can be quite chilly early morning or late evening so make sure you have warm clothing. Comfortable thigh waders are a must for serious bank fishing and a line tray on a belt is an extremely useful tool to carry.

Additional tackle for boat fishing

This style of trout fishing is essentially split between small and large waters.

Small waters
Boats on small waters almost always provide suitable anchors and it's rarely possible to drift them so the only extra items of tackle that I like to take are something comfortable to sit on and a different type of landing net. You need a fixed frame net on a long handle of at least four feet which is preferably made of wood. It won't make as much noise as a metal one when inevitably it knocks about the boat. I use a handle made of heavy cane.

Reservoir boat fishing
This demands a considerable rethink in terms of the tackle needed. The first requirement is your own anchor and rope. Although many boats are kitted out with an anchor it is usually on too short a length of rope and frequently of poor design. I have often heard it recommended that you should attach 10 to 15 feet of heavy chain to the anchor before tying on the rope so that the chain keeps the anchor at the correct angle for its arms to bite into the bottom. Certainly this works but it does make an awful noise when raised or lowered and I much prefer to use a simpler idea. I take with me a small flat weight of about 6 lb which I simply attach by a loop to the main anchor rope about 6 feet up from the anchor. This gives the correct angle for the anchor to hold. Concrete-bottomed reservoirs like Datchet or Farmoor require something a bit different as it's very difficult for a conventional anchor to hold on the smooth concrete. I have seen all sorts of ingenious contraptions in use and my idea is shown in the diagram on page 37. It works but it's noisy and heavy so I try not to move too often during a day. In addition, for reservoir boat fishing you will most definitely need a drogue. The bigger the better and fit it with a bit of rope that's thick enough to handle comfortably when pulling it in. A small 'D' shackle on the end helps for fixing it around the boat seat. Pay particular attention to your waterproofs and pack a couple of small towels. Very useful for drying your hands but also good to put around your neck as extra protection against water penetration on a very wet day. Enthusiasm rapidly evaporates when you get wet. Cold and fatigue quickly follow and no one can fish properly under those conditions. I now use

Above
A small flat weight tied in just above the anchor – simple but highly effective.

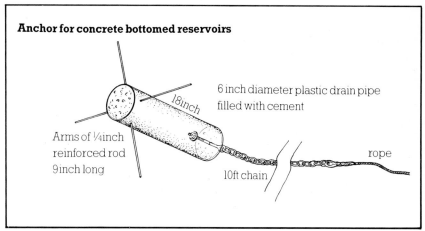

Anchor for concrete bottomed reservoirs

6 inch diameter plastic drain pipe filled with cement

18inch

Arms of ¼inch reinforced rod 9inch long

10ft chain

rope

Opposite
Bigger drogues work more effectively in slowing down the drift when searching the reservoir for signs of sizeable fish on the move.

an all-in-one Barbour type of waterproof unless I'm sure the weather is going to be warm and dry all day. Remember, too, that even on a bright summer's day the wind chill factor can make boat fishing a shivering experience even though you may well be getting sunburn on exposed skin. On the more public waters where water sports are common I often feel like some sort of oddball when returning to the jetty during the afternoon with full waterproof gear on, a sunburnt face, apart from white 'panda' eyes shielded by the sunglasses, walking past all the other people in swimwear. It's no wonder they say trout fishermen move in their own social circles – everyone else thinks we are abnormal!

That covers just about everything you actually need to go specimen trout hunting on the various types of stillwater available apart perhaps from such very specialized items such as lee boards which make a boat drift across the wind. These are not permitted on most of our larger waters and are principally used to give those whose idea of trout fishing is to tow around long lengths of lead core a more effective way of trolling.

Knots

Having covered all the items of tackle we are going to use in the methods sections, it's appropriate at this stage to discuss the various types of knots which will ensure there is maximum strength and security in your tackle set up.

The first knot is that joining the backing to the reel and I use the

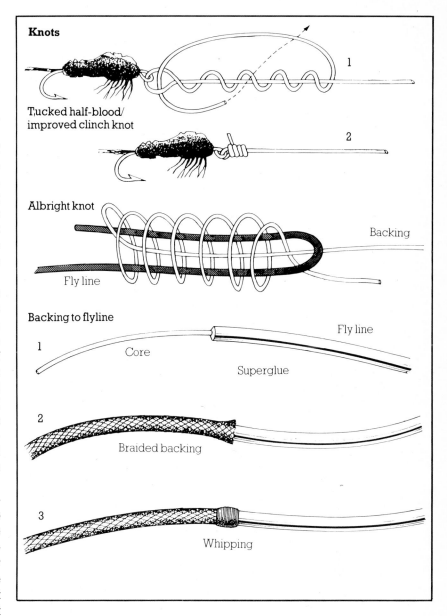

Knots

1

Tucked half-blood/improved clinch knot

2

Albright knot

Backing

Fly line

Backing to flyline

1   Core   Fly line

Superglue

2   Braided backing

3   Whipping

same one as I recommend for attaching the hook – a Tucked Half Blood. This is quite a simple knot and the easiest way to learn it is to use a wire loop and a bit of old fly line.

The next knot is for attaching backing to fly line. The Albright knot is very strong and quite simple but nevertheless is still quite a lump to have pass through the rod rings at speed and it's possible to make a much smoother joint using Superglue. You will need a piece of braided mono which is passed over the backing. Any braided Dacron type is suitable, or in the case of shooting heads you may

well choose, as I do, to use braided mono as the backing. The end of the fly line needs the plastic coating scraped off with a knife blade. You then feed this into the braid to create the smooth joint. Now lay this joint on a piece of newspaper and run some Superglue over it, folding over a couple of sheets of paper and pressing down hard for 10 seconds. This will cure the adhesive making it impossible to pull apart the joint. Trim up the frayed ends of the braided mono and if you prefer do a small whipping over each end to make the job really neat.

The knot for attaching fly line to

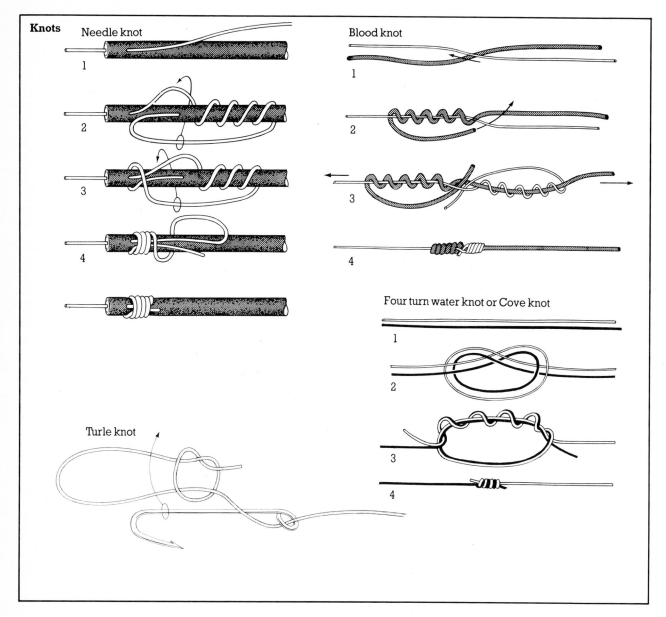

Knots

Needle knot

1

2

3

4

Turle knot

Blood knot

1

2

3

4

Four turn water knot or Cove knot

1

2

3

4

leader is often tied as a great clumsy heap which gets caught inside the tip ring. There's no need for such poor workmanship! Take a bit of care over this one and get it right! I use a Needle Knot and have found it totally secure and completely free-sliding through the rod rings. It takes a bit of practice to get lined up properly but it is well worth the effort of mastering. It's one of the reasons I carry a pin in my fly box so that I can make this knot at the water-side. Not for myself but for others. I only reckon to perform this leader to fly line knot once a year when I attach a tapered leader at the start

of the season. Apart from a very bad tangle it should never need to be replaced as I just put on new tippet lengths. If you get a lot of bad tangles or so-called wind knots then it's a fault in casting technique and a bit of cash spent with a professional instructor will help enormously. There are two simple and very sound knots for joining lengths of nylon – the full Blood Knot and the Cove or Water Knot. I use the full Blood when joining nylon down to 8 lb because it is neater than the Water Knot on thick nylon. However, the Water Knot is so simple to tie that it really is incredibly useful espe-

cially on the finer diameters.

Finally, the only other knots you need to know are for joining the fly to the leader. As I have already said, the Tucked Half Blood or improved Clinch Knot is easy to tie and very strong. The only other one worth considering is the Turle Knot although I personally find it more difficult to tie quickly. Taking my own advice I should have a few trial runs one evening. Time spent learning knots is well invested as you can be sure the day will arrive when you need to quickly make up or adapt a leader because a big trout has suddenly come on the feed.

FLIES

Every angler who delves into the world of fly tying sooner or later produces his own special pattern and it's from these experiments that we have today's vast range of flies and lures running into many thousands. The axiom 'there's nothing totally new in fishing' certainly extends to fly patterns. Synthetic materials have made changes but even the beginner's saviour – the Dog Nobbler – was first thought of many years ago and was only recently reintroduced.

My fly fishing was learnt the hard way on the streams and lakes of the West Country nearly 30 years ago when a 'twelve inch brown' was a specimen and flies larger than size 10 were virtually useless.

Those years taught me that presentation is the crucial factor in catching trout consistently. Clearly, there are advantages in using specific patterns at particular times of the year. Yet you can give the same fly to six different anglers and it will always be the same guy who takes the best bag. Why? Because he's the angler using watercraft and presenting the fly in an acceptable way to the trout.

I think that there is an amazing amount of confusion over the use of different patterns particularly with regard to many so-called imitative patterns. There are those who will have you believe that their copy looks just like the real thing but does the real creature have a rigid body or a whacking great curve of metal hanging under it? Or for that matter, a big, black shiny head with a metal ring sticking out? It's the fishermen who are being fooled by this vast army of flies. So far as the trout is concerned the flies fall into the following four groups:

Imitative The fly looks similar to something the fish regularly feeds on or has eaten before.
Suggestive The fly behaves like something the fish feeds on.
Attractors The fly looks edible and behaves in an interesting way and although the fish doesn't know what it is, he eats it.
Aggressors This group of flies either look like competition for available food or territory or else provoke sheer hostility in the fish who has only one way to deal with such an intruder – chase it and grab it.

Personal approach

These broad concepts on how a trout sees our flies were evolved over a number of years while I was spending a lot of time after the biggest and best trout from a wide variety of waters. Working out techniques to catch them meant using many different styles of fly and a whole range of sizes from minute 20s to enormous tandems until I could be sure that a relatively small range of patterns would be sufficient. This done, I could then develop my own particular approach to the many problems associated with consistently catching specimen trout.

Although I actually carry about a thousand flies for a day's reservoir boat fishing and far less – about 50 – for small clear water stalking, I use relatively few different patterns for the vast majority of my fish. As long as I'm fully confident of the fish-catching ability of the fly I have tied on, I can devote all my efforts towards showing it to the fish in an acceptable way for the particular location or circumstances.

Confidence

This is one of the major factors in being a successful trout fisherman and the pattern of fly being used often doesn't matter too much. There are anglers who only have faith in a fly if it is tied with certain materials or shades of colour and yet others who would happily fish throughout the seasons with just one or two patterns, albeit in a range of sizes. I could perhaps manage quite well with just ten patterns on the wide range of waters I fish but it would not suit me well as I very much enjoy experimenting to try and get the fish to take new patterns or improve on old ones.

Pattern analysis

When I first set out to assess which patterns had been the most successful I put together a list from memory and then set about analysing the past ten years of

The Dog Nobbler can produce trout for the novice with relative ease but you'll find watercraft rather than a sinuous tail will always win out with quality fish.

records from my diaries. The list which ultimately emerged was somewhat different to the one I originally envisaged and very much emphasizes the need to maintain an accurate record of all your fishing trips. I found that the whole range of flies had worked in convincing large trout that they were edible. Nymphs, dry flies and lures have all worked well in the many different stillwater fisheries where specimen trout can be found. I further broke down the list into the various types of waters and while there is no doubt that I spend a far greater proportion of my time fishing a nymph than any other fly, the results in terms of successful captures of specimen trout make interesting reading.

Having said that I spend most of my time nymph fishing, you'd obviously expect the majority of the fish to be caught by those tactics. But it is very interesting to see how high the percentages are for dry fly. Although the scope for using such tactics may be limited to comparatively few opportunities throughout a season, such opportunist fishing can reap excellent rewards. The daddy long legs flying period must be the prime example, but floating fry tactics in early October can also produce a few surprises in the way of very large trout. Similarly, the thoughtful use of lures can often fool an old, well-established trout into taking his last meal.

Trout food

While it is always good to see fish feeding off the surface it's important to remember that the vast majority of the food consumed by stillwater trout is located subsurface. This comprises such lifeforms as snails – ideal for growing large trout. Incidentally, it's easy to tell if the trout are eating snails. Lean over the side of the boat and listen carefully. If you can hear the fish groaning then you know they are trying to pass the empty shells! Shrimps, corixae and the many stages of insect development are all excellent growth producers but unless such creatures exist in very large quantities then larger trout in reservoirs particularly will move on to feeding on coarse fish. There is a very wide variety of insect life taken by trout and most have two or three stages to their development.

Entomology

I firmly consider that it is essential to have, as a minimum, a working knowledge of the various main groups of insects, their development stages, where and when they are likely to be found and how their behaviour affects trout. This study of insects – entomology – is a fascinating hobby in its own right and my knowledge and appreciation of the insect world has been considerably enhanced through my long friendship with Taff Price. Without doubt he is the most widely respected angling entomologist in this country and if you have the opportunity to attend one of his illustrated lectures then go. Time with him is like being treated to a living library of information.

Capturing specimen stillwater trout does not demand that you 'match the hatch' in exact imitation but you must have an understanding of the more common trout food forms. This information, coupled with intelligent observation on the day and allied to careful presentation of a suitable fly, will be more than a match for most big trout.

Choice of fly

Assuming that you have noted some activity among the trout and have made a reasoned assumption as to what they might be feeding on, how do you then choose the right fly? It's an established fact that many anglers don't even make the effort. They prefer to believe what has been written in the fishery record book and blindly use those named flies or the latest killing pattern described in the Angling Press. Others fumble blindly through the fly box or constantly swap colour and style in the mindless hope that eventually the right choice will be made and something will grab hold.

Obviously, it is possible to be a little more positive about the choice of pattern than that!

My methods vary with the type of water being fished and are best summarized by looking in

Analysis of specimen trout caught over ten-year period (percentages)			
Small waters	*Nymphs*	*Dry fly*	*Lures*
Clear water stalking tactics	90	2	8
Clear water search tactics	65	15	20
Coloured water tactics	50	10	40
Reservoirs			
Bank tactics, natural stocks	55	25	20
*Bank tactics, conventional stock	40	25	35
*Boat tactics, natural stock	30	30	40
Boat tactics, conventional stock	40	30	30

*Conventional stock implies regular weekly/monthly stockings of takeable sized fish.
*Natural stock relates to waters receiving stocks of fry only or natural regeneration.

Nymphs	Hook	Leader Strength lb (BS)
Seal's fur damsel	L/S 8, 10	5/6
Wiggle tail damsel	L/S 8	6/7
Fluo green tail damsel	L/S 10	5/6
Pheasant tail nymph	10, 12	4/5
Cove pheasant tail	6, 8	6/7
Corixa	10, 12	4/5
Sedge pupa	8, 10	5/6
Lead bug	8, 10, 12	5/6
Hare's ear	8, 10, 12	5/6
Dry flies		
Sedge patterns	8, 10, L/S 8, 10	4/5/6
Wickham's fancy	10, 12, 14	4/5
Daddy Long Legs	L/S 10	5/6
Lures		
Black lure	L/S 6, 8, 10	6/7
White lure	L/S 6, 8, 10	6/7
Muddler variants	L/S 6, 8, 10	6/7
Tandems	L/S 6, 8	6/7

(L/S = Long Shank)

land situations and have a very rich and varied food source available to their stock fish which – if they can survive angling pressure – will often grow to a considerable size. These waters demand the use of a greater range of fly presentations rather than the use of special patterns as the fish are certain to have seen almost all colours and shapes in their life.

Essentially fly selection comes down to observing the actual conditions on the day you are out at the water. Light, temperature, wind, barometric pressure and water clarity all play a part. Relate these factors to the likely food supply and then it's only a matter of fishing the fly in the right style, depth and speed of retrieve. Although this all sounds awfully complex, I aim to show that fly selection can be almost predicted.

Favourite flies

These are patterns which have been consistently successful over many years and which have often not only caught specimen trout for me but are generally recognized as excellent producers of fish on many waters. The following will form an excellent stock of patterns to begin your hunt for specimens. Each is listed against the commonly used hook size and normal tippet strength.

Lists of dressings for these flies appear at the end of this chapter with tying details, if unusual, but many can be purchased from good tackle outlets or there are a number of professional fly tyers who will make up special orders – usually for a minimum half-dozen per pattern.

When to use

Ignoring the months of December, January and February when waters are generally very cold with limited insect activity and indeed often unfishable, the flies listed are

turn at the various groupings of stillwaters.

Clearwater stalking tactics This generally requires an initial approach with a leaded pattern suggesting some form of nymph. Individuals sometimes need a showy lure to induce a take, providing the fishing regulations permit their use, or, rather infrequently, the use of a dry fly in the late evening or during unusual activity such as falls of ants or mayfly.

Clearwater searching tactics Again an initial approach with nymphing tactics is called for but this time with larger, less heavily leaded and more imitative patterns. Lures for such water also come into the imitative group in that leaded Muddlers fished very slowly can represent bullheads or stoneloach. Dry fly tactics need not be confined to specific occurrences as often larger than average fish will come up for a sedge when nothing else is happening.

Coloured water tactics This means using flies and methods to avoid the capture of basic-sized fish. Sometimes it's possible to throw anything at an individual selected from fish seen to rise but generally you need to use large slow-moving lures or nymphs and rely on confident takes from fish convinced they have found a good mouthful.

Naturally stocked reservoirs These rarely have sufficient food supplies to produce many very large trout but their relative specimens will require an approach based on their normal food items or opportunist happenings such as falls of terrestrial insects. Conventional lures rarely work – apart from days when the weather is very rough. Simple searching of the water with generalized patterns – the so-called standard wets or traditionals – will not be a method to consistently find the larger fish.

Conventional stocked reservoirs These are generally in low-effective over the periods shown in the adjacent diagram.

Fly tying

There are certain advantages to tying your own flies, not least of which is the satisfaction of catching a fish on your own creation. It does mean that you can determine the style of dressing that you prefer by which I mean, say, a slimly-dressed body or a bulky one. Also, you can put in the amount of lead which exactly suits your particular water or casting style and the overall balance of the fly can be correctly worked out. This is particularly important with larger patterns to ensure that they swim on an even keel and don't wobble or twist when retrieved. For the purposes of catching specimen trout the most important aspect of tying your own is ensuring as far as possible that the hook is perfect for the job.

March	April	May	June	July	August	September	October	November
		Seal's fur & Wiggle tail damsel						
			Green tail damsel					
Pheasant tail nymph								
	Cove pheasant tail							
			Corixa					
			Sedge pupa					
		Lead bug & Hare's ear						
		Sedge patterns						
		Wickham's fancy						
Black lure – White lure – Muddlers – Tandems								

Hooks

The fish we are trying to catch are in most instances very fit and strong and quite capable of breaking or straightening out a poor-quality hook. I use several different patterns of hook to cover the range of flies in my boxes but they must all have the ability to penetrate quickly and retain a good hold in the fish's mouth – often in areas where there is very little tissue over the bone. The older a trout gets then the bonier its mouth becomes. This is particularly noticeable with browns which also usually have far larger teeth than rainbows. I have found this out to my cost on several occasions when unhooking browns which are not quite dead. A sudden thrash and you get a series of small cuts on the fingertips and on cold days they really do hurt.

Specimen trout need a strong, dependable hook and this means either a very heavy wire or a forged bend. The disadvantage of heavy wire is that it takes a lot of power to pull it in firmly and you just can't use heavy enough leaders to do that. If you do, then the chances of getting the fish to take are very much reduced. Also a heavy wire will be more prone to wearing a hole during a long fight with the consequent risk of it dropping out when the fish leaps or gets slack line.

Points must be needle sharp at all times and the barb should be only a shallow cut in the metal. Also, distance between point and end of barb should be short so that the hook gets a quick hold without needing to be driven in a long way. Many of the flies used will also need quite a lot of lead in the dressing so this increases bulk and reduces the effective gape of the hook. We, therefore, also require hooks of wide gape. Finding

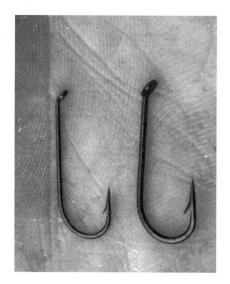

Right Excessively heavy wire and a barb, more at home on a harpoon, brand this hook as a reject. **Left** A shallow cut barb on the forged pattern means improved penetration. The gape is satisfactory and the eye neatly formed.

Captain Hamilton Heavyweights.

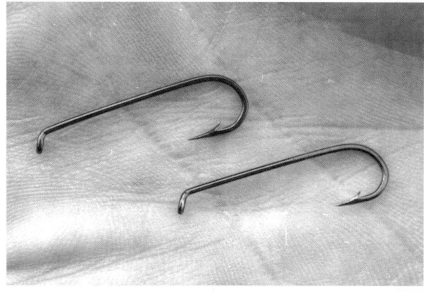

Above
Mustad 79580 with its long point (top). Better to file the point down as shown (bottom).

Right
Sproat (left) and Limerick patterns for dressing smaller, unweighted nymphs.

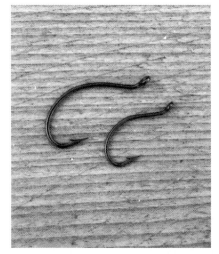

Yorkshire Sedge hooks.

patterns that exactly match all these requirements is not exactly easy even though there are many hundreds on the market. Leaded flies on standard length shank in sizes 8, 10 and 12 are the most used patterns for clear water stalking where at times very heavy trout can be encountered. My all-time favourite hook for this style is a fast-dwindling stock of Sealey Forged Roundbends but as these are unobtainable now I have been trying other patterns over the past few seasons. The current range of Captain Hamilton Heavyweights made by Partridge are very good indeed and I am also very fond of their Yorkshire Sedge hook in 8s

and 10s. Its profile is excellent for shrimp and bug patterns and I have yet to straighten out either of these two hooks. I do play large trout very hard indeed so they get a good testing. Another very strong standard shank pattern is the Mustad 7780C which also has the advantage of being slightly offset which many people consider is more effective for hooking. Its barb is rather rank but the point can be filed down a little to make it easier to penetrate and get a good hold. The Mustad 79580 is a long shank hook which is again very dependable and I use it for all my patterns which require the extra shank length. It is also available as a 79582 which is longer still and very useful for tandems. The only problem with this hook is that the point is rather long and fine. I have on occasions lost fish and then found that the point has been turned over – presumably where

it hit bone and eventually bounced out. I nowadays file the point down about $\frac{1}{16}$ of an inch to make it stronger. This is why I recommend a good file to be easily accessible in your waistcoat or jacket pocket.

Touching up a hook point at regular intervals is a good habit to develop. Smaller unweighted nymphs I tie up on Sproats or Limericks, both of which are strong hooks but do avoid fine wire patterns. If you are making your own flies then always test the hook when you clamp it in the vice by pressing down on the eye. If it bends throw it away. Sometimes you get a batch that snap when tested like this and I have always found that on these rare occasions the manufacturers will replace

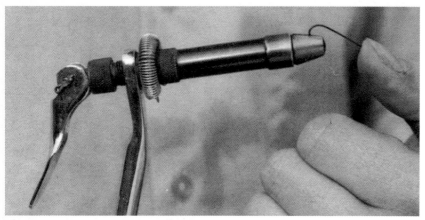

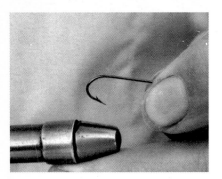

Top
Frequent touching up of the hook point with a good file is an excellent habit to develop.

Above and left
The vice test. Press down on the eye and if there's any suspicion of distortion then scrap the hook.

without question. There will always be hooks that fail during a fight but if you at least do whatever possible to eliminate using faulty ones then your chances of remaining in contact will be much improved. Flies purchased from suppliers should be checked by drawing the point over your thumb nail until it sticks in and then

give it a good pull to test it. If it won't stick in – sharpen it.

Developing special patterns

If I cover the thinking behind the development of three of my favourite patterns then you should be able to evolve your own

variants by adapting standard patterns to the method of fishing for specimens that most suits the water you finally choose to exploit.

Wiggle Tail Damsel

This pattern took quite a bit of thinking out but the initial ideas came about one windy summer day on Weirwood reservoir about ten years ago. I was bank fishing and in the waves at the edge I spotted what seemed to be little fish darting about. After a great deal of groping about I trapped one in my line tray and found to my surprise that it was a damsel nymph. Now these little creatures were free swimming at a surprising speed between weed beds and with a most pronounced wiggle of the abdomen. Up to that time my damsel pattern had been the more normal seal's fur style but it had often been taken very violently by trout, particularly so when on a very slow retrieve, and quite often it had been broken on the take. With a sudden flash of inspiration I realized that trout which were accustomed to eating damsel nymphs would be expecting the occasional one to dart off at high speed and they, therefore, take them with a sudden rush to prevent the nymph escaping. That would explain the violent takes and indeed I have subsequently confirmed this many times by watching trout in clear water fisheries. What I wanted to do was copy the wiggle of the nymph and I first tried the system of an extra length of body attached by wire loops to the main hook but this never really worked properly. A length of dyed olive kid leather about $\frac{3}{16}$ of an inch wide would, when wet, produce an ideal movement of a medium speed retrieve, but I eventually settled on a one inch tail of olive marabou tied up to an imitative body section on a weighted hook. Fished with a fast figure of eight retrieve, this fly

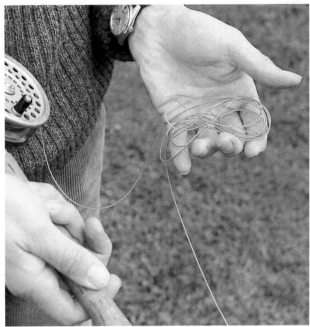

imitates the wiggle of a damsel nymph and has certainly been good enough to fool a lot of trout.

Lead Bug

Somewhat of an oddity, this little creation has accounted for eight of my double-figure trout. I noticed quite a few people using conventional flies over ribbed with heavy lead wire on the small, clear water fisheries and others who just used the lead alone ribbed up a hook shank. Obviously the fish thought

Figure of eight retrieve
Top left
Hold line in left hand between thumb and index finger. Extend remaining three fingers forward to pull back line and form loop.
Top right
Close fingers into palm of hand and trap start of another loop with thumb and forefinger.

Above left
Again extend fingers to form loop. First loop can be seen tucked into palm of hand and taking figure of eight shape.

Above right
A bunch of loops showing the figure of eight pattern which is easy to release for the next forward cast. Some anglers allow the loops to drop out of the hand on long retrieves as it is difficult to hold more than eight yards.

Left
Wiggle-tail.

Above
Lead Bug.

these offerings were edible and I started to use a pattern whereby it had a few feather fibre tail whisks, a body of lead wire, thorax of fluorescent chenille and a short hackle. The main idea of the fluorescent blob was so that I could clearly distinguish the fly in the water. It worked quite well but couldn't really be said to be at all representative and once a big fish had seen it and refused to take, it would often panic and hide after seeing it again. I then amended the pattern to be more nymph-like and yet still retain the quick-sinking characteristics allied to small size without panicking the fish. Using wool or floss thread for a short tail and building up a thorax hump in the same material, it's possible to produce a fly with a good nymph profile with the lead wire being suggestive of the abdomen segmentation. Tied in pale olive I have found that size 10s and 12s can be repeatedly shown to trout without any fear of them bolting. Indeed they will often take the fly after having refused it as many as twenty times.

Leaded Copper Hopper

This pattern is made for fishing well down in the water and slow

rates of retrieve. I had caught quite a few good trout on a variety of muddler patterns when fishing them slowly on slow sink lines but wanted something more effective. American hopper patterns were just being used in this country some 15 years ago and I started putting lead into them to fish deeper down. After trying lots of different colour ideas I eventually settled on a combination of copper body and brown wing as being very unobtrusive and yet combin-

ing the palmered body hackle and muddler head for maximum water disturbance and hence fish-attracting properties. It has picked up some good brown trout which have already had in them small ruffe or stone loach and that's proof enough that it is taken for a small bottom-living food fish just bumbling its way along.

Below
Copper Hopper.

Requirements of an artificial fly

In order to convince a specimen trout that it should accept an artificial fly it must be seen by the fish in one of the following four roles:

Imitative Here the fly must not only act like the natural model but must also be sufficiently realistic to stand close scrutiny from a suspicious fish. Size and profile are very important as is colour and the true skills of the fly tyer are needed to select materials which combined together will give an accurate representation of the creature being copied. A daddy long legs is the perfect example.

Suggestive These patterns call for a more general approach where size and colour are not too important but profile and style of fishing are the principal factors. The lead bug which is basically nymph-like but alongside a real one looks quite out of place is an example of a fly which needs to suggest a food form more from its retrieve style than its imitative ability.

Attractor This group of flies needs to attract attention by some unusual feature such as the green tail on the green tail damsel. In other words, factors which make a fish investigate or take notice and are sufficiently attractive to make the fish think they must be edible even if he isn't fully sure just what is being eaten. Colour and size are important features in attractor patterns and retrieve styles can simulate life.

Aggressor This is the straight lure

type of fly where garish colour or excessive size and movement make the fish want to attack the fly because it's seen as competition for territory or food. Most anglers will be aware of the rainbow trout's reaction to 'hot' orange. Why do they grab such flies so aggressively? I know that it's often written that they take an orange lure in the summer because they are feeding on dense clouds of daphnia but that only applies to reservoir fish and such lures work just as well in any sort of water. Although excellent trout are caught on all sorts of weird creations I don't rate aggressor-type flies as being sufficiently consistent to warrant using in the hunt for specimens. I know that there are exceptions to every rule but I've found that my flies and tactics have had a better overall performance against large trout than anglers who always use flashy lures.

Materials

I'm quite convinced that all fly tyers have far too great a range of materials just as coarse fishermen have a vast array of floats but it is useful to have materials which act in different ways. Feather fibres, be they from quills for nymph bodies; downy style as in marabou

for mobility; cock hackles to hold up a dry fly; or hen hackles for movement in nymphs and wet flies; all have uses for different flies or parts of them. Just as various hairs and furs behave differently or give alternative effects, so it is necessary to make use of the properties of all materials commonly used in fly tying to achieve the required effect in the fly for whatever purpose it is required. Careful choice of material can greatly enhance the ability of a pattern to do its job and examples of this are using polypropylene for dry fly bodies because it is slightly buoyant and repels water. The lead bug uses floss silk instead of feather fibre to help it sink faster without requiring excessive lead and the black lure uses marabou wings for maximum mobility when retrieved slowly. It's all a matter of thinking very carefully about what the fly is intended to represent to the fish and whereabouts in the water you want it to fish.

Lead

Weight in my fly dressings is essential to most of my patterns and the way in which they are fished. Lead wire or strips of foil from wine-bottle tops is always in my tying kit and in the list of

Two large lures removed from the mouth of a trout with my smaller nymph tying pictured alongside. The fish had become extremely suspicious of fur and feather but it was outwitted by careful presentation.

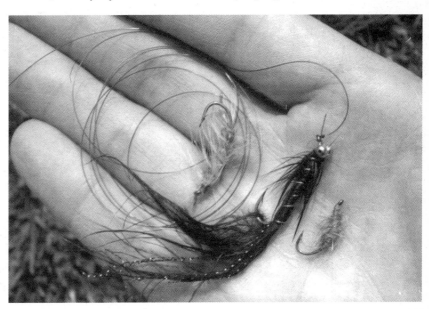

dressings (see page 55) I have put the rough length of fine lead wire or its equivalent that I would advise be incorporated against each hook size. Be wary of using too much lead until you are used to casting weighted flies.

Tying a Seal's-fur Damsel Nymph

Selecting an 8 or 10 longshank hook (Mustad 79580) clamp into the vice and twang the eye to test the hook's temper. Using a spool of waxed thread – preferably olive – hold the end in your left hand and take a few turns up the hook shank towards the eye and return back so as to attach the thread to the hook. Cut off the waste end and now tie in the end of a length of lead wire or lead foil. I would generally use about four inches of wire and three inches of foil at $\frac{1}{8}$ of an inch wide. Tie this on very securely to the hook keeping it all up towards the eye so as to avoid filling up the hook gape or else stack it up on top of the shank to form a hump. Now run the tying thread down the hook to the start of the bend and tie in a half inch long bunch of approximately twenty fibres plucked from the side of dyed olive hen hackle. Catch in a four-inch length of fluorescent green or yellow thread. Next comes the fun bit of dubbing on a body made from a mixture of three different colours of seal's fur. You will need medium olive, hot orange and bright blue in a proportionate mix of 4:1:1. There are a variety of ways in which seal's fur can be dubbed, some being very mucky as when using liquid wax, others very complex with ingenious tools. But you only need fingers and this is the simple way to overcome a problem which many fly tyers just cannot cope with. Taking a pinch of seal's fur, roll it in the palm of one hand with your fingers until it forms a crushed ball of fibres about the size of a pea.

The next stage is to tease it out to form a loose web of fibres about $\frac{3}{8}$ of an inch wide and from 1–2 inches long. Lay this web on top of the tying thread and trap the end fibres against the hook shank with the thumb of your left hand. With the right hand twist the web of fibres around the thread in a clockwise direction and always maintain tension on them with the middle finger in between further twists with thumb and index finger. A rope effect will quickly form and you can then take a turn of thread around the hook to trap the end of the rope and then wind to form the body. Take another couple of twists of the rope for every few turns of it around the hook shank. This really is a very easy way to dub any fibre and if you get any sort of bother with it just wet the thumb and forefinger when doing the twisting. That just helps to bind things together a bit better. You can put on as little or as much fibre as you like and with practice it's quite possible to dub the whole body of a long shank 8 pattern. Build up a tapered body then tie off about $\frac{1}{8}$ of an inch from the hook eye. Now rib up the fluorescent thread in the opposite way to the body winding. This has the double function of trapping the fibres more securely and also it does not disappear into the body material. Try to aim for about seven turns of the ribbing material in an expanding spiral. This gives a very realistic and neat effect. Now tie off the ribbing thread and tie in an olive-dyed speckled partridge hackle. You can tie it in by the tip or stalk and then take one or two turns of the hackle around the hook and tie off. I find it easier to use my fingers but most people need to use hackle pliers, especially on these short, weak feathers. Finally stroke the hackle fibres back along the body and do a whip finish. Clear varnish if you wish, but with waxed thread and a whip finish it's not necessary.

Tying a dry sedge

I love dry sedge patterns and thoroughly enjoy making up some of the complex and quite beautiful American patterns, but we only need to consider one style for this type of fishing and providing it's made up in a few different colour combinations and sizes it will cover all our stillwater sedge requirements. Let me run through one of my favourites.

We need a long shank 10 Mustad 79580 in the vice. Any colour tying thread will do but green is best. Tie on the thread as before and put a butt section of fluorescent green floss about $\frac{1}{8}$ of an inch long just around the bend of the hook. Next, tie in an olive cock hackle by its tip and then dub on an olive body of polypropylene fibres. There are lots of brands available. Stop this body about two-thirds of the way up the shank and palmer up the cock hackle. Tie off and make a neat base for the next stage which is to attach a wing of hair fibres. I use Impala or Gazelle body hair. Take a small bunch, maybe $\frac{1}{8}$ of an inch diameter of fibres, and tie on with a pinch and loop. Try to get the tips of the hair projecting just beyond the bend of the hook. Trim off the hair in a tapering cut and wind thread over it. Now tie in two red game cock hackles by tip or butt and wind on to form a good bushy hackle, before completing with a whip finish. This is a relatively simple fly but treated with a paste-type floatant it will pop back up even if pulled under during a gentle ripple.

Tying a tandem lure

This is again quite a simple fly to tie but involves the making of a tandem hook linkage. I start off by putting an 8 long shank in the vice and then cut off about four inches of braided monofilament and thread down its core a length of nylon of about 20 lb breaking strain. Attach the tying thread to the hook and then push braid and nylon centre through the hook eye so that it lies along the underside of the shank. Try to arrange it such that about $\frac{3}{8}$ of an inch of nylon is along the hook with a further $\frac{1}{4}$ of an inch of braid beyond. Now tie this very securely to the hook shank and then begin building up the tail fly of the tandem. Let's do a simple all-black version. Tie in a short tail of black hen or cock hackle fibres followed by about two inches of fine black chenille. Wind this up to within $\frac{3}{16}$ of an inch of the hook eye and tie off. Tie in a long fibred black cock hackle and take three or four turns round the hook. Tie off and then press it back along the body and wind over the fibres so that it slopes backwards. Tie off – this is a bit tricky with a couple of inches of mono sticking out over the eye and it can only really be possible to do a whip finish by hand. Now put a new hook in the vice identical to the first and attach the thread. Lay the braided mono/ nylon combination along the top of the hook shank and very firmly tie on. Now repeat the tying process for a tail and body before adding a wing of calf tail fibres dyed black and long enough to reach the end of the tail hook. Finally another long-fibred black cock hackle tied on in the same fashion to slope backwards and a whip finish completes a very trustworthy, neat tandem arrangement.

If you use the thinking behind the tying of these three flies and follow the tying detail for the other recommended patterns then there is no great difficulty in compiling a stock of effective patterns so that the specimens can be caught.

A list of my top ten most effective flies with a brief resume of their most successful methods of presentation is not too difficult to put together but I would add that it is not in any order of effectiveness as the patterns cover a wide variety of waters and techniques.

Top ten flies

1 Black Lure

The fly that probably accounts for more fish than any other throughout the country and yet has stood the test of time and will kill the most innocent stockie or the wiliest old brown. Fish it slowly for the best results with larger fish. If trout are

Black and White lures.

moving well in the top couple of feet of water then fish it as slowly as you can with a floating or intermediate line. Ignore little knocks and wait for a slow confident tightening of the line. The same retrieve is the tactic to use when fishing deep with a sinking line and used like this it never seems to frighten fish. Keep the presentation quiet and persistent and quite often a crafty old fish that has watched it many times will creep along and take it very positively.

2 Green Tail Damsel

Somewhat of an oddity. It might be likened to a Viva variation of a standard nymph. This is a fly with two principal uses for specimens, one being for coloured waters where it needs to be retrieved very slowly on a sunk line and the other for clear but very weeded waters where it works extremely well when fished fast across the top of the weed. Fish seem to just explode out of the weed and chase it. If it's a small fish all you have to do is stop retrieving and it will refuse the fly.

3 *Pheasant Tail Nymph*

Tied up in the fashion of Arthur Cove's impression of a giant buzzer I have often used it to induce takes from large trout seen taking buzzers in the late evening but ignoring conventional imitations. Pitched in front of their cruise path and pulled quickly in front of their noses the fish will often hit it hard. I can't get it to work selectively on specimen fish when slowly trickled in along the bottom, but it will certainly pick up an excellent bag of fish when used in this way. The more traditional tying of a Pheasant Tail nymph with a tail and ribbed abdomen and slightly built-up thorax with a wispy hackle is such an excellent representation of many nymphs. I use it on trout which are being fussy about other flies and find it works well on browns in small clear water fisheries. I used it once to great effect at Chalk Springs Fishery in Sussex. This is a clear water location which besides holding excellent rainbows also is noted for quite beautiful browns. These often become

Cove Pheasant Tail (left) and Standard tying (right).

very difficult to catch and one quiet day there I found a fish which bolted every time it saw a line or fly. I noticed during the course of the day that it generally returned to the same little gravel bar so I let a size 12 Pheasant Tail slowly settle on the gravel with the fly line and leader also lying along the bottom. Leaving the rod tucked into the rushes I waited for the fish to come back and settle down. After about ten minutes I gently moved the line causing the little fly to creep slowly across the bottom. The trout promptly tipped up and sucked it in. That's an example of using ordinary flies under unusual circumstances to fool a fish that otherwise just won't respond.

4 *Daddy Long Legs*

This is a lovely insect and guaranteed to bring fish to the surface when it hatches at its best in September and early October. It's again comparatively easy to make a good bag of standard-sized fish with this fly but to catch the better specimens you need to be very observant. Watch carefully for signs of a large fish rising. That doesn't necessarily mean heavy splashes – the largest fish frequently makes a ring like a minnow but the giveaway is a lot of water movement under the surface. When you find such a fish, put the fly out carefully so that it doesn't spot the leader and it should be yours. My 7 lb 12 oz brown was just such a fish, barely making a noticeable rise form against a scum line in a corner of the lake. He sucked in the Daddy

without so much as a ripple. The tied form should be the one with trailing legs and which sits in the surface film. It then looks drowned and is easily taken, whereas one

sitting on top of the water with legs spread out will more often induce a splashy rise when the fish first tries to swamp the fly. It's very easy to mess up the strike like that.

5 *The Copper Hopper*

Much like a muddler one might say but with some unusual differences. The leaded underbody makes it sink slowly and the body hackle coupled with the deer-hair head sets up a lot of vibrations when retrieved slowly along about a foot off the bottom on a slow sink line. A good fly for larger clear waters, coloured waters or dam walls on larger reservoirs. I have caught some superb grown-on rainbows from Queen Mother Reservoir, Berkshire, on this fly when fishing it along the concrete edges about ten feet down. You will often feel a series of light knocks followed by a heavy pull and then find on netting that the trout has the fly in the back of his throat. I think they take it so confidently that the little knocks are the fish swallowing the fly.

6 *Seal's Fur Damsel*

Nothing very special about this fly but, again, you must fish it very slowly. Notice how often I repeat the need to fish virtually all my flies as slowly as possible. That way you avoid attracting smaller more suicidal fish, you don't frighten big ones by excessive casting and the takes are normally unmissable. Fish the damsel around weed beds or to individual fish if the water is one where you can spot them. Be prepared for violent takes when using this fly and hold the rod at right angles to the direction of retrieve to allow for a bit of leeway when the fish takes.

7 *Tandem Lure*

You might well think that this is just the job for confirmed lure strippers and certainly it will catch all sizes of fish. Without wishing to repeat myself it must be fished at a crawl – very slowly – for good effect among specimens. Limited in use to reservoirs as most smaller waters do not permit the use of tandems, this is a fly best fished in the depth range of 5 to 20 feet. Again it often induces a lot of light taps with the firm take generally coming as the fly lifts away from the bottom at the last stage of retrieve. Tied up as a large white muddler I have taken good fish off the top at fry time but find its best use for cold windy days when a figure-of-eight style retrieve across the wind direction and about four to five feet under the surface will pick up excellent grown-on rainbows. One frosty November day I once caught three browns over 5 lb from Queen Mother on this fly and regrettably had to put them all back as they were out of season!

8 *Lead Bug*

As I have already mentioned (see p. 47) this is a suggestive fly for use on trout which can clearly be seen and which would otherwise spook if shown something larger or more gaudy. It needs to be pitched in front of, or to the side of, fish and drawn away from them in a series of foot pulls. You can tell immediately if a fish is interested and starts to follow. Whatever you do, don't stop the retrieve or it will refuse the fly immediately. This fly will rarely frighten a trout and is very useful on ones that have already been hooked and lost.

Lead Bug (left) and Hare's Ear (right).

9 *Hare's Ear*

Tied sparsely and with ribbing before a thorax bulge, this fly is again suggestive of all manner of nymphs. That said, I tie it fat over a lot of lead and don't rib it or make any shape other than a blob of fur. When fished to trout spotted in clear water it should be moved much as the previous fly but will very often catch fish on the drop. Quite what they take it for I just don't know but I would not want to be without a few when stalking trout in clear water fisheries. It's also a very good pattern for dibbling through holes in weed mats as described on page 68.

10 *Dry Sedge*

The final pattern in my top ten list of flies which have caught specimens, is another dry fly which although not used a great deal continues to account for a good number of trout especially when cast direct to fish seen rising. Another use is on hot, still days on the smaller waters, whether clear or coloured. When it seems there are no fish around I put out a dry sedge with the end three feet of leader degreased and just let it sit by a weedbed. Half an hour is a long time to just let a fly sit but it's a tactic which will sometimes bring up a really good trout on an otherwise hopeless afternoon. In clear water I have watched them circle under the fly and disappear for a while but keep returning as though curious as to what it is sitting there. Like a cat their curiosity sometimes gets the better of them and another fish is in the bag.

Sedge (left) and Wickham's Fancy (right).

Summing Up

This list of flies is by no means exhaustive but if used intelligently along with the others I have named and maybe your own particular specials there's no doubt they will catch specimen trout. Apart from certain specialized instances I don't believe that it's the pattern which catches the fish. There is much more to fly fishing than just using a known pattern of fly. Confidence, presentation and style of fishing coupled with a full awareness of the fish and their environment will be the deciding factors and the choice of fly to match the tactics – described in the following chapter – should become much clearer.

Dressings

Wiggle Tail Damsel
Hook – long shank 8 with 2 inch of lead wire
Tying thread – rewaxed olive
Tail – olive marabou, 1 inch long
Body – first two thirds medium olive seal's fur ribbed with yellow thread or gold wire. Final third, dark olive seal's fur with thorax covered with olive feather fibre.
Hackle – long fibred olive hen
Head – olive thread

Fluorescent Green Tail Damsel
Hook – long shank 10
Tying thread – prewaxed olive
Tail – three strands fluorescent green wool 1 inch long
Body – medium olive seal's fur, ribbed yellow thread
Hackle – olive hen
Head – two balls of gold bead chain for weight

Pheasant Tail Nymph
Hook – 10 or 12 with $\frac{1}{2}$ inch or $\frac{1}{4}$ inch lead wire
Tying thread – prewaxed brown
Tail – 4 strands cock pheasant tail fibre
Body – pheasant tail fibres ribbed with copper wire
Thorax – pheasant tail fibres over hare's ear fur
Hackle – short fibred hen greenwell
Head – brown thread

Cove Pheasant Tail
Hook – 6 or 8
Tying thread – prewaxed brown
Body – from part way round hook bend pheasant tail fibres with copper wire rib
Thorax – pheasant tail fibres over round ball of dubbed blue under fur from a rabbit
Head – brown thread

Corixa.

Corixa

Hook – 10 or 12
Tying thread – prewaxed brown or olive
Shell back – natural black squirrel tail
Body – dubbed seal's fur mix of light olive, naples yellow, fiery brown. Ratio 3:1:1. Ribbed brown thread
Hackle – single turn long fibred hen greenwell

Sedge Pupa

Hook – 8 or 10 preferably Yorkshire sedge pattern
Tying thread – prewaxed brown
Body – medium swannundaze in translucent amber over fluorescent orange floss ostrich herl
Thorax – two rear-pointing cock pheasant tail fibres then a bulge of brown polypropylene with cinnamon feather fibre over
Hackle – speckled brown partridge
Head – brown thread

Hare's Ear

Hook – 8, 10 or 12 with about 2 inch of lead wire
Body – dubbed hare's ear mixture

Wickham's Fancy

Hook – 10, 12 or 14
Tail – red game cock hackle fibres
Body – flat gold lurex with palmered red game cock hackle and opposite wind of gold wire
Hackle – red game cock

Daddy Long Legs

Hook – long shank 10
Body – brown green polypropylene dubbing
Legs – ten double knotted cock pheasant centre tail fibres tied as a bunch
Wing – cree hackle tips tied sloping back
Hackle – short fibred red game cock

Black/White Lure

Hook – long shank 6, 8 or 10
Tail – black cock hackle fibres
Body – fine black chenille
Wing – in three stages along body, generous black marabou tufts
Hackle – long fibred black cock tied swept back
Head – black varnish

Copper Hopper

Hook – long shank 6, 8, 10. 3 inch fine lead wire
Tail – ⅛ inch loop of copper 'goldfingering'
Body – copper 'goldfingering' with palmered red game cock hackle
Wing – brown squirrel tail with slips of oak turkey over but tied flat
Head – spun deer hair clipped tight with ends trailing back

Sedge Pupa.

SMALL STILLWATER METHODS

Small water fisheries can loosely be defined as ranging in size from about an acre to maybe 30 acres and which generally do not cater for the stock to grow on by any appreciable amount. But where angling pressure is light it is possible for trout, particularly browns, to prosper very well in quite small waters and I'll examine the possibility of catching specimens from this sort of lake later in this section.

Waters which stock with the aim of a quick return on the fish are normally less than ten acres and can be managed in such a way that the average rod catch and average size of fish is carefully controlled. If the hatchery source is on site then stocking is done daily but more often on a once or twice a week input if the fish are bought in from outside. The number and size of fish in the water can then be accurately controlled and adjusted to suit seasonal variations such as rod numbers and weather. Most day-ticket waters are at their busiest in the March to early June and September to October periods and therefore stock according to the required average rod catch. But the weather can greatly affect the feeding patterns of trout. Even small waters of an acre containing maybe 100 fish can go right off for a few days and give anglers the impression that there are no fish in the water. Settled periods of warm weather with heavy weed growth often demand a much heavier stock of fish than would otherwise be required for the numbers of day rods. Conversely, when cover is

It's calculated that double-figure rainbows cost about £15 to stock which gives you a clue to the value of this four-fish catch totalling 51 lb 6 oz. I set a new limit record with this Avington haul which comprised specimens of 16 lb, 14 lb 14 oz, 11½ lb and 9 lb.

sparse and the water cold during winter, the trout will sometimes be so easily caught that stock levels can be very low.

Waters operated on this frequent stocking principle are the ones most likely to introduce specimens as there is then an excellent chance of them being caught fairly quickly. No fishery manager is happy when large fish remain uncaught in his lakes for weeks on end. It's imperative that they show in the catch returns. At current market prices a double-figure rainbow can cost at least £15 to stock and it needs to come out quickly before it loses too much weight or becomes almost uncatchable. Don't believe stories of such fish actually growing on in small waters. It was often said that doubles in the small chalkwater fisheries of the South could well grow on to 20 lb. Even assuming that there is a water with such unbelievably rich food sources, the trout would have to feed so heavily and consistently that it would inevitably be caught before it had much opportunity to put on weight.

Fisheries stocking with reasonable numbers of above average fish hold a special fascination for me. I know it's often said that these fish are easy to catch but the same argument applies to all sizes of stock fish and you only need to visit one of the clear water fisheries to observe how difficult the average angler finds it to catch even the basic-sized fish, let alone the larger ones. There will always be suicidal fish but they usually adapt rapidly from a stewpond environment to the semi-wild.

It never ceases to amaze me how quickly a fish learns to ignore whole groups of artificial flies and yet has only ever seen food pellets durings its three or four years of life. Fisheries which stock with a fair proportion of specimen trout in gin-clear water are my favourite haunts. Ideally, they should also

have lots of weed and bankside cover. It's waters like these where I can target individual fish.

Stalking

This sounds an odd expression in a fishing context but it sums up exactly what I like to do. I simply walk the banks looking into the water to locate a large fish – and then by observing its reactions and behaviour try to catch it on a small

In growing-on pools rainbows are cascaded with a daily diet of pellets – but once released they can become infuriatingly selective in what they eat.

nymph. When a real specimen finally decides to accept my fly then that is the moment I find the most exciting. If the day ever comes when I no longer feel a special thrill when a big mouth

There's gin-clear water and bags of bankside cover at Chalk Springs fishery near Arundel making it possible to target individual fish.

shuts on my fly then I shall move on to another aspect of the sport. I know I'm still hooked at the moment because my Polaroids keep steaming up at the critical moment!

The simple approach

Stalking tactics demand a lightweight approach as I can often cover several miles of bank in a few hours and most certainly don't want to be carrying around a load of tackle. All my requirements can be carried in the pockets of a decent waistcoat with a large sliding frame net slung on my back. Rod, hat and Polaroids and I'm ready to go. I found that a satchel holding the smaller items of tackle

was a nuisance to carry and sometimes got left on the bank but more often it was a hindrance in getting the landing net quickly into action. Carrying a long handled net is also a bit of a pain as it must be picked up and put down with every change of position. I was forever leaving mine lying somewhere along the bank and then being forced to land a big fish by hand.

Keep your tackle requirements to a minimum, wear comfortable clothing for the weather expected and be prepared to do a lot of walking. Mobility is so often the key to locating and catching a large trout from the small clear water fisheries. You can never be sure just where to locate these better class of trout, although familiarity with a water will give you a pretty shrewd idea of where the favoured marks are likely to be throughout the year. Once a fish worth catching has been located it's almost certain to remain in the vicinity. But rainbows are great wanderers and you can never really be quite sure where one will go, especially if it gets spooked by a flashy fly or a splashed cast. Many times I have walked slowly down a lake behind a row of anglers studying the progress of a large trout as it passes through holes in the weed. When it finally settles down it will hopefully see my fly for the first and the last time. The need to observe trout behaviour led to the need for carrying the minimum of equipment so as to be fully mobile in pursuit of clear water specimens.

Polaroids

The most important accessory you will ever purchase is a good pair of Polaroids. These make an enormous difference to your understanding of fish behaviour and are absolutely indispensable for clear water stalking. The basic lens principle is the same whether they be made of plastic or glass. They are now available to prescription if you normally wear glasses.

Polaroids cut surface glare by eliminating most of the ultra violet rays. In practice this works best when the sun is high in the sky from about mid morning to late afternoon. It doesn't matter how good your glasses are if the sun is low in the sky and this is of particular importance now that winter fishing is commonplace. Lens colour is a much discussed topic but

the consensus among experienced water watchers is that brown/amber is the best colour for most light conditions while grey is marginally better for dull days or when there is a lot of surface disturbance from wind or water movements. Those which give everything a yellow look are really at their best for looking into white water on rivers.

Subtle approach

I have previously mentioned the need to dress sensibly for this and indeed any other type of fishing. It's important to blend into the background so do avoid very bright clothing or strong contrasts between items. The same goes for hats; after all that is the tallest part of you and even if the rest of you is hidden by bankside vegetation it's not much good having a white hat bobbing about for the trout to panic about. Keeping a low profile can be a very positive advantage but it does seem that today's angler wants to stand bolt upright on the edge of the water in full view of the trout and yet still expects the fish to come right in close and confidently take his fly. It's true that in the majority of small clear water fisheries there are not many old hands about and that it's rather easy to deride the occasional eagerness of newly introduced stock. Nevertheless, fish which have seen nothing other than the earth or concrete surrounds of a succession of stewponds seem able to very rapidly revert to type and assume all the characteristics of wild grown fish. Just you try catching a big trout that has survived a couple of weeks in a few acres of well fished water. It's not too difficult to summarize the principal faults of people who really want to catch a big clear water trout but repeatedly fail to do so. Foremost is lack of observation coupled with an incorrect balance of tackle which leads to poor pre-

sentation of the fly. Even if things do go right and a specimen trout moves to the fly, panic then sets in and the retrieve is either stopped or vastly speeded up and the fish promptly refuses the fly. Assuming it takes and the fly isn't immediately whipped out of its mouth, most anglers then seem to let it run for a few yards before clamping down hard and neatly breaking the leaders. Actually getting to the netting stage is pretty rare but even that is fraught with danger when a big trout is being attempted to squeeze into a floppy little net. It's amazing how loudly nylon breaks when a heavy trout flops out of the net half way out of the water. In all seriousness, if you do come across a specimen in clear water just stay calm and give yourself time to work out the best approach. Once the fish is on, keep the rod well up and put on as much pressure as you dare. Providing the hook remains in then the fish should be yours.

Assessing specimens

Where it is possible to look into the water and spot the trout it takes a lot of practice to accurately assess the size of a fish. Obviously, the best way of gaining experience is to look at lots of different fish and catch a few so as to make comparison between appearances and true weight. However, it's possible to shortcut this by first of all watching trout in hatchery ponds, where this is permitted, and having an experienced angler confirm your assessments. Then treat someone you can trust to a ticket on a good water and ask them to go round with you pointing out the various sizes of fish. Water depth, light angles, condition and sex of the fish can all be variables in making it difficult to accurately judge the size of a trout.

Incidentally, it's not uncommon for algal blooms to break out on clear water fisheries. These algal

The special thrill of a big mouth closing on a fly – in this case a 20 lb 7 oz record-breaker and size 8 Hare's Ear!

blooms colour the water and make it very difficult to spot the fish. But don't knock the fishery – it's a natural phenomenon triggered off either by the water warming up in spring, sudden very heavy rainfall or the periodic build up of nutrients, all allied to the amount of sunshine. Perhaps I can also lay to rest another myth – that of cock rainbows being treated as second rate. I will admit that at certain times of the year – dependent on the strain of fish – cock rainbows will be grey, flaccid creatures often exhibiting fungal growths on spawning wounds. When caught they promptly spew milt everywhere and go very black when killed. This is only natural. There is absolutely nothing wrong with

their flesh; it's only their outward appearance which is at odds with the customary silver bright fish. I think the American nickname of 'chromer' is perfectly apt for a fish in peak condition. If the water you fish tends to stock with out of sorts cock fish, speak to the manager.

It's quite possible to select reasonable looking fish at all times of the year and unless a hatchery has bungled its stock assessments by holding too many cocks it ought to be capable of supplying clean fish all year round. Most thinking hatcheries dispose of their cock fish in August/September when they are in perfect order. You won't often come across a particularly large cock fish. Hatcheries have found that they are not much use for breeding purposes beyond about 5 lb. As they grow bigger cock rainbows become less proficient at achieving good fertilization and, as a mild winter can cull cock rainbows by as much as 30 per cent, it just isn't worth keeping them into old age. This situation only applies to small waters with a rapid turnover of stock but if you do find a good sized cock fish then try to get him as the fight is frequently very tough indeed.

A large cock rainbow can be often recognized by a slightly protruding lower jaw which can appear to have a square end. It's very easy to be misled over their size as they can be very deep in the body – a factor which is not easy to observe when looking down on a fish. I can well remember my best cock rainbow. I was after a fish I thought to be in double-figures when the fly was violently taken by the big one's companion, a fish I thought to be about 5 lb. I really worked hard to hustle it in quickly so as not to spook the bigger one. But, I just couldn't get it to the net and had a tremendous fight from what proved to be a cock rainbow of 9 lb 4 oz. When I finally landed it I had

The prominent lower jaw of a Duncton Mill brownie which seized a dry Sedge on a late summer's evening.

made such a commotion that the other fish had gone. That serves as a classic example of how to turn up the chance of catching a specimen by incorrect observation. I could so easily have pulled away from that beautiful fish.

Choosing a victim

Most of my time on a clear water fishery is spent wandering the banks searching for a sign of a better than average fish. It's difficult to say exactly what size fish should be singled out as you could devote an hour to a difficult one of 5 lb only to have missed a chance of a much bigger rainbow a little further along the bank. If I know the fishery well then I usually have a quick look in recognized holding areas. If there is an exceptional fish in one – say 5 lb plus – then I will try for it. If it doesn't come out quickly I leave it for later and carry on assessing what is available in the water that particular day.

Within an hour I usually have a pretty good idea of what is about and then decide which fish to go for. But if nothing of interest is showing I then carry out a very thorough search of every likely spot, looking hard for fish that may have been previously hooked and are behaving quite differently to fresh stock.

What to look for

A large trout cruising near the surface will be quite obvious and most anglers will be able to judge that it is well worth pursuing even if they may be several pounds out in their initial size assessment. But trout lying at the edge of weedbeds, under overhanging bushes, deep in the water or in positions where the light angles are bad or the surface disturbed can be very tricky to estimate. Often you will only see part of the fish or possibly just a shadow. There are several ways of assessing the size of these problem fish. First, look for other trout in the vicinity and wait until they are in a comparable position to the possible target so you can make a judgement of relative sizes. Secondly, you can spend time studying the fish to get a

better view of it or move position to improve the viewing angle. I often move from side to side or up and down in an effort to find the best light angles from a given spot. The third tactic needs a lot of confidence and involves casting to the fish. Hopefully it reacts and comes to look at the fly. You then keep retrieving in such a way that it has to chase the fly until you can get a good look at its size. Now comes the tricky bit. If it's a big fish reduce the rate of retrieve allowing it to catch the fly without becoming alarmed, or else pull the fly away very fast so that it loses sight and wanders off. This action avoids the fish coming too close to you and possibly spooking. Once it has turned away cast again and this time do a slower retrieve to induce a take. There is a useful dodge here to catch a big fish that follows but won't take. Change colour pattern and get the fish to do a fast chase. When it's within ten yards lift the rod rapidly to pull the fly very quickly out of the water. Chances are that the fish will turn on the spot looking for the fly. Cast it straight back on top of the fish and it will very often be taken immediately.

Brown or rainbow?

Although these two fish look very different when out of the water it is not always easy to tell them apart when seen from above. Usually, a brown will appear yellowish and when it turns will often flash a dull gold and its bigger spots will show up. Perhaps the most obvious difference is in their behavioural characteristics. Browns are very territorial and will dominate a particular area of water, rarely straying far. The fact that they tend to stay much lower in the water than rainbows means their feeding habits are not so easy to observe. They definitely do not fool easily. A large brown in a small clear water fishery will frequently be seen feeding and actively moving but will completely ignore all artificials. Whereas a large rainbow can sometimes be goaded into taking a fly, a brown must be *persuaded*. Rainbows feeding well, usually travel in an elongated, circular route while browns normally adopt a figure-of-eight patrol and do so at a much more leisurely pace than their flashier relative.

Both species will lie quite still at times and again it is possible to seemingly wake up a rainbow by showing it a succession of flies but a large brown will steadfastly ignore everything.

A feeding fish

Watch a trout for a while and you can soon tell if it is actually feeding. One that is pushing into clumps of weed and then snapping about is clearly flushing out insects and eating them. A trout that cruises purposefully and keeps turning slightly to briefly open its mouth is also actively on the feed.

Don't be misled by occasional fish you will see – usually within a few hours of stocking – that swim very fast in an aimless way all over the lake. These are orientating themselves with their new surroundings and will take time to settle down. Also, be wary of a fish slowly cruising along and appearing to rise. If it then releases bubbles as it swims off only to repeat the performance a short time later then it again is not feeding but simply adjusting itself to the water after a trip in the richly oxygenated water of a hatchery truck. This phenomenon is called 'topping' and is much more noticeable in some waters than others.

Trout lying quietly alongside weedbeds or under bushes may not necessarily be obviously feeding but providing they don't instantly bolt when shown a fly there is an excellent chance of inducing them to take.

Will it take?

Nymph fishing

It's not easy to describe the appearance of a fish that is likely to take a fly but it will give the impression of being more alert than another in that its fins will all be raised. The fish will move in sharp, little twitches when it is about to take. It's more noticeable with very large trout and I often describe them as appearing to bristle all over at the sight of a fly and indeed you can sometimes see them shudder slightly before coming after the fly.

Surface fly fishing

Where the fish is taking surface fly or you want to try and get it to take a fly off the top, then slightly different characteristics are shown. You sometimes find good fish lying in weed which is quite impossible to fish through with a nymph because it would rapidly snag or get covered in fine algae. This is the time to put out a dry fly and wait for the fish to find it. If the trout is cruising about in the weed then find a fairly clear section, cast the fly into it and wait for the fish to find it. Again, if the trout appears to be very alert when it spots the fly then you are sure of an offer. If the fish circles under the fly then it's suspicious. A slight tug on the line to make the fly twitch will sometimes bring an immediate response.

If the trout you have found is not moving about then make a very accurate cast to place the fly lightly about three feet in front of the fish's position. Let it settle for a few seconds then give it a twitch. If that doesn't make the fish show interest, give up and simply wait for it to move.

Rising trout

Despite what some people will have you believe, there are days when even the very biggest trout will rise and this frequently hap-pens on small, clear waters if the fish are not being thrashed at by lure merchants. Early in the season, pond olives will frequently get the fish up at around midday and it's very much a matter of selecting a good sized tying and being very accurate with your casting so as to avoid water disturbances and also the likelihood of an unwanted fish taking the fly. Spent mayfly will also bring up the big fish and waters such as Damerham in Hants are well noted for this exciting style. Also, a dry fly is sometimes the only way to fool a large brown in the small clear waters. Quite why this should work is puzzling but I know of several good browns caught in this way and have often used the technique myself on difficult fish.

Presentation

This is the crux of the matter in specimen trout hunting and there are tips worth following to help get it right without frightening off the fish. First, don't be in a rush to cast as soon as you spot a big fish. Have a good look at its behaviour and consider if you are in the best position to cover it. There may be weed between you and the fish which would prove unlucky if the fish decided to follow the fly for a long way before possibly taking. It's not much good if the fly runs into weed after only a few yards – the fish won't be fooled like that again. Don't cast at the fish from behind unless you have no other option. A fly retrieved back towards a fish will first of all allow it to see the leader and also it's a bit unusual for any water creature to literally ask for trouble by directly approaching the fish. Far better if the fly is moving across its path or away from the trout.

Some fish will react to the plop of a fly entering the water and will immediately turn towards it. You must then keep moving the fly to get it following for the take. Stop moving the fly and the fish will almost certainly refuse. I like to cast so that the fish I am after only sees the fly and keeps its attention on that alone. For that reason I try to cast about three to four feet in front and maybe six to ten feet beyond the fish. That way it should see the fly enter the water and if it turns to look it gives me a reasonable distance to move the fly in its path so as to get the take. Don't expect really large trout to pounce on the fly. I have had many a double just amble along behind the fly and then slowly open its mouth to take.

Depth

Judging the depth at which a chosen fish is swimming is not easy because of the very nature of the crystal clear fisheries. The water gives the impression of not being very deep and consequently fish lying say eight feet down may only appear to be two or three feet below the surface. This is extremely important where very large specimens are concerned as I have found them to be most reluctant to rise up in the water towards a fly. It has to be presented at their level, hence the need for a bit of lead to get the fly down quickly and to keep it there.

If you fish unleaded or very lightly weighted flies then just cast into the water and watch how long it takes for the fly to reach the bottom. Repeat that procedure with a big trout and it may well move off. Even assuming it does hang around until the fly finally gets down deep enough it will probably have had a good look at it and then as soon as you start to retrieve to put some life into things the fly starts to rise up in the water. You must keep the fly at the fish's depth – this is vitally important.

The take

Let's asume that a reasonable cast

has been made, the fly is quickly down to the fish's level and the retrieve has started. Following the fly is a single very big fish, keen to eat the morsel that has suddenly appeared in front of it. Swimming along behind the fly and facing the angler it opens its mouth and engulfs the fly. A rapid strike and one very puzzled fish hurriedly leaves the area wondering why its meal suddenly shot out of its mouth. It's so easy to strike before the fish has closed its mouth or turned its head. *You must wait, and time the strike to perfection.*

I find this the hardest part of catching small water specimens and have many times been guilty of striking too soon. If the fish is pointing right at you when it takes then lift the rod straight up to make the strike. But if it turns its head to either side or points its head down then strike by pulling to one side. Either way you must wait until the mouth is shut and that can be a very long time indeed with some fish.

Playing smallwater specimens

Where it is possible to pursue fish with stalking tactics I try to get them to take my fly as close in as possible, even if that means making it really chase after the fly by pulling it away when it goes to take.

That might sound somewhat risky but it generally makes them all the more positive when the fly is finally taken. The advantages of hooking the fish at close quarters are that you can sometimes hustle it into the net before it is really aware of being hooked, but principally it gives you the upper hand during the fight. Although I only use five or six pound leaders it's not difficult to hold double-figure trout to within ten yards of the rod top by never letting them get their head down. Once you panic and let a big fish run then you will

Opposite, top
With a big trout close in under the rod it can be very tiring to keep up the pressure.

Opposite, bottom
But you can achieve extra lift and power by positioning your left hand up the rod.

really be in trouble, especially if there is a lot of weed about.

Big fish hooked at much beyond ten yards will usually run a long way no matter what you do, and the best defence is to hold the rod as high as possible to keep the line out of the water and free of the weed. As soon as the fish wallows on top apply side strain and get it back to you as quickly as possible. With a big trout close in under the rod it can be very tiring to keep up the pressure on it and this is where you can achieve extra lift and power by putting your left hand about two feet up the rod. As soon as the fish shows signs of rolling on the top get the net out and pull the fish over it. On many small waters there will be a lot of surface weed mats and fish will frequently get enmeshed in them. This is no great problem as once their head is covered in weed they stop fighting, but you now need the strong rim of the big net to push it through the weed and under the trout.

Don't expect to be able to lift out a trout much over 5 lb in the net. Just lift the rim clear of the water and drag the fish into the bag of the net. Now you can use the rod hand to grip the net shaft and lift it all out onto the bank. You must now immediately kill the fish and a good solid priest is essential. Mine weighs 12 ounces and nothing argues after being hit with that!

Difficult trout

The most difficult trout to catch are often those holed up under weeds or bushes after being pricked or

Opposite, top
As soon as the fish shows signs of rolling on the top get the net out.

Opposite, bottom
If the trout's head becomes covered in weed it will stop fighting. Push the strong rim of the circular net through the weed and under the fish.

Right
Finally, lift the rim clear and drag the fish into the bag of the net.

Below
Hook a fish at close quarters and you can sometimes hustle it into the net in double quick time.

Dibbling at the rod end in a tiny clearing among the weed.

hooked by another angler and are very suspicious of things that go plop in the water. Those under weed mats can sometimes be induced to come out by dropping a fly very accurately at the edge of the weed and slowly retrieving it. They are almost always very reluctant to move far from cover and unless they take within a few feet will turn back.

The better method is to lower the fly from the end of the rod and jig it up and down at the edge of the weed. Better still is to make a hole in the weed mat with the rod top about four inches square. Lower the fly into this hole and move it up and down. Regrettably, you won't see the fish take but will suddenly have the rod top dragged down. Trout much over 5 lb

are very difficult to land like this if you let them run and again the best tactic is to immediately get the fish on top and let it thrash the weed away before slipping the net under it. This hole in the weed technique is called dibbling and can be very successful on hot, bright days when the better fish have taken cover. Trout which have been in the water some time are very reluctant to chase a fly and are much like those lying under bushes. They need a careful approach. I try to work out their limited patrol and get a fly into the water without them seeing it enter so that the first time the fish spots the fly it is moving through the water. This is where the little lead bugs and Hare's Ear nymphs are so effective. They don't frighten the fish and can be shown to the same trout many times. These very difficult trout will sometimes only take a fly after they have seen

it many times. However, if they become at all agitated leave them alone for a while and then try a different fly.

Time wasters

These are trout which have either not settled down or have been badly frightened or indeed may be ill. A fish swimming around so rapidly that it is almost impossible to intercept is not worth bothering with and neither is one that is idly swimming along with its fins all closed in. These latter types can look very sullen and very often have a fly in their mouth from a recent encounter. Trout which immediately dash away when they see a fly or are lying perfectly still on the bottom are also going to be really hard work and I only bother to go for these types if there is nothing else about that is worth chasing.

A day at Avington – a typical small stillwater

Let me run through a typical day on my favourite fishery to give you an idea of the problems which can occur on a normal day's stillwater fishing on a small set of lakes.

All the rods for the day set off for the lakes at nine am by which time I will be fully kitted up with a fly on the rod. If it's a good bright day I will normally start off with a size eight leaded Hare's Ear or similar. Cloudy or rainy days call for a fly with a blob of fluorescent material in its make up. The first lake is long and narrow. Assuming that it's mid-August when weed growth is at its most luxuriant then there will be little point in looking for much in the first 50 yards. About halfway down the lake by the sedges is a deep channel and it's well worth a look in this section. The bottom quarter of the lake is well known for its fairly easy, early fish and several rods stop off here. Unless I can spot a good one I give this area a miss for an hour or so. On to the second lake and a careful walk all the way round finds a good number of two to three pound fish with a much better looking one in the widest area near the lake head. This fish is well out in the lake and is cruising around with three others around the 2 lb mark. Because it's a cast of about 15 yards I quickly change the fly to a smaller, lighter lead bug because it's not at all easy to control the heavier fly in the air at that range.

First cast and one of the small fish rushes over and takes the fly on the drop. I do nothing and wait to see it spit the fly out after much mouth snapping. A fast retrieve to clear the area brings one of the other two pounders hurtling after the fly. I let this one come right in close before quickly lifting off and putting the fly about ten feet in the path of the better fish. As the nymph sinks I see the trout turn

slightly towards it and immediately start to retrieve in foot pulls. The trout ambles up to within six inches of the fly and follows it for several yards before turning away.

I let it return to its previous area and this time cast well beyond it so that a faster retrieve brings the fly quickly across its field of vision. That does the trick and it quickly accelerates up behind the fly. A big white flash of mouth and firm upward strike followed by a leaping, crashing fight brings a super 5 lb rainbow to the net. It is hooked just behind the inner plate of teeth in the top jaw. On the stringer, pop it back in the water and off I go again. Walking down towards the third lake I see other standard sized fish being played and one angler tying up a new leader. He tells me he saw a beauty which took immediately but has broken his three pound tippet in dense weeds. Yet another big fish lost through fishing too fine for the type of water and size of trout. Moving down to the third lake I find that the light is not yet high enough to look into the deep hole apart from around the edges and all I can see are a couple of two pounders. Down through the middle section of the lake are a couple of nice looking fish moving slowly in and out of the weed. They look to be around three pounds but my first cast snags floating weed and the fish disappear at the disturbance caused. Under the trees at the far end is usually a good spot and today there is one of around four pounds patrolling under the branches. Changing the fly to a small Hare's Ear I wait for the fish to come my way and then drop the fly in off the rod top. He darts forward grabs the fly and with a quick lift I'm into an interesting situation, with very little room to move the rod among the trees and a very angry trout on the end. Best course of action under these circumstances is to put the rod top

underwater to get it free of the branches and tire the fish right out. This one comes in without too much difficulty and I then take a slow walk back up to the head of the lake. Three anglers fishing here, all aiming for the middle and stripping back flies rather in exess of the fishery limit of l in. When will they ever learn? Looking along the edge under the bushes I find a good trout of maybe seven or eight pounds lying quietly near the bottom. Takes one look at the nymph sinking towards it and disappears. Up to the second lake and a slow look. No sign of the big fish reportedly lost earlier but out in the middle of the widest section there are a couple of fish rising and one looks well worth catching. Quite a long cast here into pockets of weed so I put on a lightweight version of the lead bug but with white floss so I can spot it. This fish is a difficult one because it keeps disappearing in the weed. After about 30 minutes I get it all right and it takes the little nymph on the drop. I do love hooking a big fish at long range in weed so it's up with the rod as high as possible and play it off the reel for a while. Chap on the opposite bank gets a bit upset when I ask him to stop casting at my fish which is wallowing near him. Great fun this battle but once in close under the rod top she is well beaten. Weighing 7 lb 12 oz! I'm now very pleased with the bag of fish. It's not every day I pick up trout of this size and despite what a lot of people may claim you will do well to catch maybe twenty or so over 5 lb in a season going maybe once a week. Three good fish on the stringer and now up to the first lake to have a go at the fish which sit in under the trees. One is a clearly visible cock fish of maybe $2\frac{1}{2}$ lb trying to chase off anything that comes his way. I can't see anything larger around so I try to get him out. It takes a long time and several fly changes before I can work out he

Hotspot action in the first lake at Avington where scores of giant rainbows have fallen over the years.

will at least look at black ones. On with a black, lead bug but with a fluo green tail, mini Viva? He chases in hard to grab the fly in shallow water. Typical of cock rainbows he fights really hard and gives the impression of being much heavier but $2\frac{1}{2}$ lb was a good guess. Lovely bag of fish and it's only 12.30. Sometimes I go for the additional two to make up a summer limit by spending some time on the stream but manager Roy Ward hasn't made a profit out of me today so it's off home to cut the grass instead.

Larger clear waters

These fisheries of maybe over twenty acres frequently stock excellent specimens and may even have some grown-on fish if angling pressure is low. As you won't be able to use stalking tactics on such waters there are two basic approaches towards getting out a high proportion of the specimens. One I call opportunist fish-

ing where you must take maximum advantage of infrequent or unusual conditions which may induce large fish to temporarily lose their caution. The most obvious instance is when insect activity is such that the movement of surface feeding trout will enable an accurate assessment to be made of the weights of individual fish. Judging the size of a trout by its rise is not easy unless you can spot some part of it breaking surface. The most usual is to see the whole or tip of the tail. Falls of ant, hawthorne, mayfly, daddies or abundant terrestrials will sometimes bring about these circumstances. The trick here is to develop the ability to scan a wide area of water and resist the impulse to cover fish feeding well, until it's possible to sort out one that is much better than the rest. Obvious places to concentrate on are near weed beds and overhanging bushes. Big trout like to have cover nearby. Don't expect to see a huge splash. Big fish will, if they have any sense, expend the minimum amount of energy that is necessary in acquiring their food. I got a beautiful brown of 4 lb 6 oz one hot afternoon by putting a small sedge over a rise form that looked to be

no larger than a minnow. When a lot of fish are moving you must be very patient and try to work out the patrol route of the biggest before ever putting out a fly. You can often see a lot of underwater disturbance associated with quite a modest surface rise and that is a sure sign of a big fish. This opportunist fishing can also be used if, for example, you spot a large fish showing just once. You need to develop the ability to lift off and very rapidly cover the fish. This sort of one-off cast can produce what I call bonus fish where I simply take advantage of a suddenly presented opportunity. Continuing with opportunist fishing is the situation where trout will feed on fry of small coarse fish species. Don't assume that this only occurs at the back end of the year. Some smallish waters have large numbers of sticklebacks which are heavily preyed on at three stages during the year. One is at their breeding time in the spring when a large pheasant tail nymph works particularly well. Secondly, when the fry are shoaling in midsummer at the pin head stage on the edges of weedbeds and then again in October when weed growth is dying back and shoals of semi adults form up. Once again careful observation will often give you the location of a large trout chasing the little fish. These are generally the longer established trout and most certainly won't get caught by a casually thrown lure. Watch what the trout is doing and plan accordingly. If he is only having a go at the fish every 15–20 minutes then wait until his feeding period is about to start before starting to fish. You must always assess ways of presenting your fly to maximum advantage when trying to hook specimens and the old adage 'a fly in the water for the maximum possible time will give the highest score' is not necessarily so when after large fish. Often just one cast has been enough although I may not have fished at all for the previous half hour.

Visible activity from large fish due to specific circumstances will give many opportunities for the observant angler but most days there is little sign of life from the larger trout.

Searching larger clearwaters

Big trout tend to favour certain parts of lakes and the most obvious will be dam walls, deep water and heavy weed cover. Unless you have gleaned some local knowledge it will pay to concentrate efforts on these areas. It's not possible to spot specimen fish by sight, so you need to employ tactics which in the main will avoid the smaller fish. The largest fish in a group always seem to act differently from the others, even if it's a couple of two pounders in with fish running at 4 oz each or a double figure trout in with a lake of two to four pounders. The larger members of a group seem to hold themselves aloof from the habits of the smaller individuals and are less inclined to snatch at anything that moves. Working on that prin-

cipal you need to fish slowly and steadily and wait for really positive takes. I find that it is best to use lines of intermediate or faster sinking rates dependent on the depth of water to be fished or where I want the fly to be. Water up to six feet deep is comfortably fished with an intermediate density line and the fishing depth of the fly can be altered by having a series of dressings with differing amounts of lead in them. Bear in mind that the retrieve will almost always need to be very slow and therefore even a slow sinking fly could be well down in the water after a 20 yard retrieve. Flies for fishing in such clear water lakes need to be of a reasonable size and the Copper Hopper, Black or White lure or Damsel Nymph will all collect their share of fish. Use a minimum of a 5 lb point and a leader of at least 15 and preferably 20 feet. Casting needs to be efficient, i.e. as far and as delicate as possible. This avoids too much water disturbance and it also very much pays to fan the casts so that the same section of water is not being repeatedly covered. I find that takes from the larger fish are either a sudden heavy stoppage of the line where you are taken very positively, or else they develop as a series of light plucks which very gradually tighten up into a solid draw.

Where the water is known to hold good browns which may well have been in for several years then the retrieve needs to be very slow and as deep as possible. Contrary to the normal expectations of large water browns. I have had quite a degree of success with small water browns in the heat of the day during summer by repeatedly bumbling a muddler along the bottom. Quite often the fish will surface as soon as it hits the fly and it usually comes as quite a shock to see a big brown on the top at the same instant as you feel a pull on the line.

Coloured water tactics

Many fisheries in clay or acid run-off areas are either permanently coloured with clay suspension or peat stain and consequently are impossible to look into. Although the fishes' vision must be restricted by some degree they still respond to flies in much the same way as in clear water fisheries. As a general rule I would advise that you very carefully search the edge of such waters even if it means either casting along the bank or sitting down away from the water edge so that the retrieve can be carried through right into the shallows. The larger fish in these waters seem to be more prone to patrolling the edge and I think this is often why complete beginners with very limited casting ability will connect with large fish. However, if you use the slow and steady methods and don't strike at every little pluck you will average out pretty well with the better class of trout. The Green Tail Damsel can be surprisingly effective during the summer months in these waters and works better than the standard Viva in getting a better proportion of the specimens. One other method which can produce the larger than average trout is to fish a dry Sedge. Let it sit in the surface film out over deep water and don't move it for as long as you dare. I have picked up several 5 lb plus fish from waters like Willinghurst in Surrey by patient use of this method. Persevere with the slow methodical approach. It's better to end the day with one four pounder every second or third trip than an endless succession of also rans. By now it should be clear that one fly at a time is all I suggest you use. The whole aim is to concentrate on the presentation and control of a single fly. Besides which if you go putting on droppers you'll just tempt unwanted small fish.

RESERVOIR TECHNIQUES

Apart from being more at the mercy of the elements, reservoirs are set apart from smaller stillwaters by their stocking programmes. Where fishing pressure is relatively light because of poor access or competition from other waters in the locality then some reservoirs can sustain a superb level of sport with injections of fingerlings alone. And, if there is a suitable feeder stream, it's even possible for the reservoir to partly rely on natural propagation for brown trout. I'm convinced it's also possible on rare occasions for rainbows to reproduce successfully, given the right winter weather. I recall watching shoals of beautiful little rainbows of 3–4 inches on Stithians in Cornwall some years after it opened when stocking was still with 12 inch fish. This type of water is not rich in food but is quite capable of growing fish on, to two or sometimes three pounds with 12–16 oz being a pretty fair average.

Contrast these waters with reservoirs which are stocked with the size of fish more normally seen in small waters. Here the water may not offer the food resources for fish to grow on to any appreciable size or angling pressure may be so intense that few survive long enough to pick up weight. Such waters, termed Grade 1 Fisheries in the South West, are stocked with a base weight trout of 12 oz to 1½ lb and a sprinkling of larger ones.

There is a further type of reservoir where the water is very much richer. These are located where lowland chalky areas have been flooded, and there's enough food for fish to grow on quickly. Also, once a water reaches a few hun-

dred acres in size it will offer sufficient space for a proportion of its trout to elude capture and to put on a substantial amount of weight. Again generally operating on a base stock size of say 1 lb–1 lb 8 oz, or slightly more as with the Bristol area reservoirs, these reservoirs can expect fish to reach 2 lb–2 lb 8 oz by late summer. If the trout

Above and right
Heavy marginal weed and a barbed-wire fence descending into the deeps of Bewl Water in Kent are just the sort of features to inspire confidence. I cast to a hefty surface-feeding rainbow but hooked this rather smaller fish that rushed in first to grab my Sedge.

survive another season they may well reach 4–5 lb and considerably larger if they make it a further season.

Exceptionally rich waters such as the Queen Mother Reservoir can grow rainbows to 10 lb plus and in 1986 Bewl Water in Kent peaked with large numbers of 7–10 lb fish following a period two years previously when it stocked a great many fish approaching 3 lb. The survivors of these stockings had such a good start in life that

they did very well indeed. The actual percentage of large, grown-on fish is really very low in proportion to the total annual catch and it's necessary to look very closely at ways of cropping them successfully.

It wasn't many years ago that reservoirs relied on a two or three times a year stocking of their base weight fish. However, greatly increased fishing demand meant that for many months of the season it was extremely difficult for the

average angler to catch his fish. This led to the introduction of trickle stocking with fish introduced at weekly intervals, or even less, throughout the season. Trickle stocking has been greatly simplified by the use of net cages suspended over deep water where small fish are reared on to the release size and are already accustomed to the water. This system ensures that the reservoir always has a good proportion of new, relatively easy to catch fish with a proportion of each batch growing on to give a wide range of potential weights.

Instant specimens

Some reservoirs release brood fish early in the season and that inevitably guarantees a burst of big-fish publicity. There are also many other instances where good-sized hatchery-reared fish have been introduced to boost attendances. The release of large fish into vast acreages of water must inevitably be a very risky business and a lot of them are probably never seen again. Nevertheless, it's an accepted part of modern trout fishing although I have no idea how to go about catching these fish. It's all down to luck.

Overwintered trout

Now these are an entirely different proposition and in some waters could represent an appreciable number of the actual total stock. It is widely believed that rainbow trout do not survive the winter but looked at logically that cannot be so. They survive in hatcheries so why not in the wild? In truth, there are very few *cock* fish that get through the winter in the larger waters and that is also true to a lesser degree in hatcheries. Where they are hand stripped the survival rate is quite good but a mild winter can often bring about 50 percent mortality of held-over

Comfortable thigh waders and a line tray on a belt are key items for the serious bank angler.

give a good indication of the potential for locating grown-on fish. After that it's all a question of selecting the right method.

Deep water – lead line fishing

The use of lead-cored lines trailed behind free drifting boats or those with specialized rudder control has led to some exceptional catches of prime, fast-growing trout on the larger waters. Much has been written of the effectiveness of these tactics when coupled with large lures incorporating the rubber tails of sea fishing baits. Certainly this style crops off the mid range of naturally grown fish but it is rare for the water's largest trout to be caught using these methods.

Most of the really big Rutland, Grafham and Queen Mother specimen trout have been taken by boats at anchor or by bank fishermen. It's my belief that if trolling were banned then the stock of specimen trout in some waters would increase. By trolling I mean all tactics where lead lines are operated from behind moving boats. Fish caught in this way cannot possibly show their paces and it's just a way of freezer filling. Much more credit goes to the guy who catches specimens from an anchored boat or the bank where lead lines are legitimate tactics.

Reservoirs – boat or bank?

There are two main factors to consider when deciding whether to search for specimens by going afloat or fishing from the shore. The first is the whereabouts of the bigger fish and the second is the

cocks. Of all the grown-on reservoir fish that I have had over 4 lb I can only recall one that was a cock fish. That one was 4 lb 12 oz from Queen Mother Reservoir and was so unusual that I recorded it separately in my log of specimen trout.

I firmly believe that a good proportion of rainbows in all waters come through the winter but they may well lose weight rather than gain it. Many waters are just not capable of growing on trout and unless the residual stock are fed during the close season they will be in poor condition come the spring. However the richer reservoirs which promote rapid growth in their trout will produce excellent specimens.

The position with brown trout is somewhat more complex as these fish live considerably longer than rainbows and do not appear to have any problems surviving the winter. That's not to say you won't catch browns that are in very poor

shape early in the year when they can be almost eel-like. This happens in even the richest water and frequently in a hatchery environment. For some, as yet unknown, reason they suddenly go back in condition and rapidly lose weight. Cocks are much more prone to this phenomenon than hens. Again, there are reservoirs which are well known for consistently producing numbers of specimen browns. Obvious examples are Rutland and Grafham. Other waters might yield exceptional specimens like Queen Mother and Farmoor. There are also reservoirs which seemingly ought to produce numbers of good browns but fail to deliver. Here I am thinking particularly of Bewl Water, Kent. This reservoir does give up the odd good browns but it's rarely worth the effort of pursuing them.

Most reservoirs publish accurate catch returns and these will boat hire which can triple the cost of a basic bank ticket. This can amount to as much as an average man's take-home pay for a day and although one should never equate a day's sport in terms of cash value it is nevertheless a relevant feature of reservoir fishing.

Leaving aside cost considerations I would say that the chances of catching grown-on reservoir fish consistently will be better if you regularly use a boat. It's true that at certain times of the year in certain hotspots the bank angler will locate excellent trout. But usually it is the boat angler who can search the water more effectively and take advantage of the conditions on a particular day to maximize the chance of catching a specimen.

Boats and their use

Day-ticket reservoirs are nowadays mostly equipped with fibreglass boats which are available with or without engines. While I really do enjoy rowing as an exercise it can turn a day afloat into a bit of a grueller if the wind is at all strong. Given the choice I always take out a motor boat – I must be getting old! But many reservoirs offer only pulling boats for hire and you must therefore take heed of conditions on the day before planning your fishing area on the water. If you cannot row too well then do not attempt to go a long way downwind only to be faced with a hard pull for home at the end of the day. Similarly, you should check the weather forecast, taking particular note of wind strength and possible changes in direction. This is not quite so important when the boat has an engine but basic rules of seamanship must still be followed. For example, you must not turn broadside to large waves or you'll be in danger of swamping. Also don't run into a strong wind too fast or the boat will crash into the

waves too heavily and you risk damaging tackle and overturning. Life jackets are always available on public reservoirs and while it is not always mandatory to wear them it is most certainly advisable. Most reservoir managers will not allow their fleet out in strong winds and will call in all boats if the weather forecast suddenly worsens. There are many small but important points relating to the use of engines, not the least of which is that you must not engage drive with the engine revving or the shear pin will break. This can also happen if you run into shallow water or thick weed. When lowering or lifting the anchor don't let the engine lift clear of the water when on tick-over as it will no longer be drawing in water to cool it and may seize. Don't tie the anchor or drogue to the boat rowlocks as this can impose a lot of stress on the boat in a strong wind – tie up to the seats. In essence you must be conscious of the fact that being dumped in deep, cold water when wearing full protective gear will give you a very short period of time in which to reach safety. Incidentally, wearing waders in a boat is the height of stupidity. Much more practicable are short waterproof boots with leggings or trousers.

Fishing at anchor

I'm sure that most anglers believe you must fish deep when at anchor but I use quite the opposite tactics moored in one position. The most important thing to do when anchoring is to ensure that it holds the bottom in the position you choose. An anchor will only effectively hold if the angle between it and the boat is very low so that it can dig well into the bottom. A simple, folding grapnel type of about 10 lb weight will hold a boat in most winds if used correctly. Many people attach great lengths of chain to them so that the angle of

bite is kept low down. I find it less noisy and more convenient to just make a loop in the anchor rope some ten feet from the anchor and tie on a flat weight of around 7 lb. If you don't want to go to the expense and bother of carrying your own anchor then this simple weight idea will effectively convert most anchors supplied with the boat into effective tools. The rope needs to be positioned carefully to ensure that the angler or anglers can fish effectively. The most comfortable way for two anglers fishing is to tie the rope to the centre seat. However, this puts a lot of wind pressure on the boat's side and can cause it to make the anchor drag. If this is the case then much less resistance is set up by tying the rope to the bows. To make it more comfortable for two anglers to fish, the rope can be brought down the side of the boat gunwhale for a couple of feet and held by a G clamp. This holds the boat at an angle to the wind, enabling both anglers to cover the water without one always having to retrieve up alongside the boat. Fishing at anchor means you can only search an area in a 30-yard radius from the boat. Fresh fish could always move into range, but you are essentially covering the same group of trout in that vicinity with every series of casts. Any disturbance in the boat will certainly put those target fish on edge and make them suspicious. Poor casting technique in calm or light ripple conditions will also keep fish away from the boat. Rocking of the boat when casting is caused by using the shoulder instead of the arm and although the line may shoot a good distance, it's physical force not technique that is achieving this. Simple etiquette is sadly missing among anglers on most reservoirs but is it really so difficult to avoid motoring in front of another boat or anchoring up within 30 yards of another?

Drift fishing

Unless the wind is very light, drifting before the wind will generally be too fast for effective use of the methods I advocate. Similarly, the use of rudder control or lee boards (where permitted) is not very effective at connecting with large fish when used in anything other than a light breeze. This technique of moving a boat across and downwind can also be very confusing to others if there are a lot of boats on the water. Any drift fishing that I do is always with the use of a drogue attached to the centre seat. Depending on the size of the drogue in use it's possible to almost stop a boat in a moderate breeze and if fish are freely moving in the upper layers it's a very effective way of presenting the fly to as many as possible. However, unless you're prepared to make full use of opportunist fishing to observed individuals then it isn't a really suitable way of searching out the bigger fish. Throughout this book I describe methods to enable the fly fisherman to consistently catch the larger trout from a particular water; these are not methods to catch quickly large bags of the basic-sized fish. That's why some of my strategy seems totally at odds with accepted trout-fishing dogma.

Reservoir hotspots

As I said in the chapter on small water tactics, there are areas in all waters where the larger trout will tend to congregate. Therefore, when faced with perhaps several thousands of acres of reservoir it's vital to have at least some idea of where to begin your search. The same criteria apply to most reservoirs except the concrete-bowl type which have their own peculiarities. I would certainly recommend that you choose one or at the most two waters to concentrate on. That way you will more rapidly learn the varying requirements of each water depending on the conditions. Frankly, on reservoirs over a hundred or so acres I choose an area or arm of water and fish there exclusively until I feel that I really know it well enough to perhaps take a gamble on another area on a day when nothing seems to be happening. That approach and the intimate knowledge gained has given me the confidence to be patient and wait for circumstances to change and bring the fish on the feed. Quite often in a full day out you may only get a half-hour period with any realistic chance of picking up a good fish. It's no good having completed a limit of small ones for the sake of some action when a little patience could have produced a single, really memorable fish. That said, there are recognized hotspots on all reservoirs where there is a better chance of catching a specimen. But I have a sneaky feeling that these hotspots develop simply *because* they've become a favourite fishing patch for anglers in an otherwise featureless expanse and so get more attention than elsewhere. Big fish will never be far away from good food supplies.

Feeder streams

Where streams enter a reservoir there is invariably a deeper channel and this provides excellent cover for big fish to lie in wait ready to ambush shoals of small fry or to feed on whatever is carried down in the current. Sometimes, too, the incoming water creates a localized environment different to that of the remainder of the reservoir and this can give rise to particularly heavy weed growth harbouring a lot of insect life or perhaps extensive snail beds feeding on detritus washed down by the stream. Some species of coarse fish love to swim in a current, particularly at or just after spawning time, and a big old trout soon learns where to find them.

Promontories

These are found at the points of bays or where a long section of land protrudes into the reservoir and act as collecting areas for food carried by currents set up by wind action. These currents can be surprisingly strong and I can remember once fishing Queen Mother Reservoir in a strong blow when a cast downwind with a Hi-D head would be swept back towards the boat once it had gone down about ten feet and so fast that it was difficult to keep pace with the flies. The other useful feature of a promontory is that the angler positioned on it can command a wide area of water if bank fishing. However, a boat anchored off shore where the water deepens will often be the best spot during a steady wind, particularly if it has been in the same direction for several days.

Drop offs

Anywhere the water suddenly deepens will always be a holding spot for large fish. They may not necessarily feed there as available food at such points is not normally much good but it gives good cover for a fish to lie up between feeding spells. Again, it's a matter of playing the waiting game until fish move out to feed.

Fixed structures

These include marker buoys, boat pontoons, fish cages and draw off or inlet towers. All act as attractor points for small fish and also give cover for large trout to lie in ambush. I have had days anchored within range of a marker buoy when the only good fish to show or be caught have been within a few feet of it. Boat pontoons with their trailing weed growth and shade act as a magnet for shoals of fry, in much the same way as towers, and will always be visited at some time during the day by a few big trout. Floating cages are an obvious holding area for specimens because of the easy feeding available

under them when the stock is fed. I doubt that the fish in these areas will ever be effectively cropped because of the need to keep boats out of casting range to prevent hooks getting into the meshes and consequently risking injury to the men who have to handle them when grading and stocking operations are taking place.

My home-made stringer which incorporates a carrying handle. Suspending the catch over the side helps ensure the trout remain in good condition.

Wind lanes

Rather an odd phenomenon which definitely acts as an attractor point for actively feeding fish. It's nice to do a slow drift along wind lanes picking up fish that show but to contact the occasional specimen it's far better to wait until the wind lane goes over or past a known holding area and then anchor to the side of it. That way you can watch for signs of a large fish moving into it. They will often only cruise a wind lane for a few yards before dropping down to return to base and make another run through. Observation is again the key and this is an ideal point at which to lead on to identifying big trout just by the rise form.

Assessing size among rising fish

When trout move to feed on a stage of insect development on or just below the water surface, it follows that the bigger they are the more water movement there ought to be and therefore one would assume that the biggest splash is made by the biggest fish. However, in practice this doesn't work since the bigger the fish the slower its movements and the less energy it will waste in obtaining food. Subsurface feeding is the most difficult form of feeding in which to assess the size of a trout but it can be done by looking for a hump in the water, caused by the fish turning, and a boil just behind it. The size and length of duration of these two features will give an indication of the weight of the fish causing them and, once again, it needs experience to fully assess this. Surface feeding on buzzer pupa is a nice easy way of sorting out the bigger trout as this is a real giveaway when they break through with head and tail. I usually watch for tails and start by picking on those that seem to waggle as they submerge since these

are usually quite a long fish. I then try to watch one individual before finally deciding if it's worth going for. Believe me it is a very difficult thing to just sit in a boat or on the bank when trout are rising freely. The temptation to hook something is almost irresistable but you really must just wait and watch. Trout taking adult flies off the top do so in a variety of ways according to species but can be roughly grouped into three.

Small flies

Small flies such as olives gnats and the like are taken very quietly by the bigger fish and the rise form to look for is the one which makes very little surface movement but is accompanied by quite a good-sized underwater boil. In calm conditions you often hear such a rise but can't locate it until you realize that it's coming from a single ring like a minnow coming up. I love it when the artificial fly is taken just as confidently as the natural one.

Sedges

Sedges are quite a mouthful and like moths are taken positively because the fish is either afraid of it taking off again or has had to chase it across the surface. This gives a very substantial water movement and you need to look for a heavy swirl often accompanied by a small spout of water. Good sedge hatches are not as common as I would like but one small water with a regular occurrence is Ned Kelly's, Duncton Mill in Sussex. I spent a lovely evening there once when all I wanted was a good brown and I was able to pick out a fish from dozens of trout taking sedge. As the light started to go the brownie gradually became more confident until he slurped down my sedge.

Larger flies

The larger flies such as Mayfly and Daddies are taken very leisurely

The white line marks the wind lane in which will be all sorts of food – plus accompanying trout. Across the blue waters of Farmoor Reservoir in Oxfordshire is a valve tower which almost certainly draws in the browns.

by large fish in an almost exaggerated rolling movement. It's essential to develop the ability to scan large areas of water and detect any sign of movement. This will then enable you to pick out fish at long range and work out the first indications of a good-sized one on the move. Big flies on the water will almost always give the chance to spot a good fish but you can't rely on seeing one at close range and must be constantly alert to the possibility of spotting a big fish feeding. A favourite way for the larger trout to feed is to select only spent or drowned flies so that the minimum of energy is used in taking them.

When the larger flies are on the water it pays to look for slack areas just out of the wind where the surface is a little scummy. Here you will sometimes see very small rise forms accompanied by a bulge in the water. That will be a good target fish but it will need a careful approach so as not to disturb it. You should plot its patrol route and place a fly in its path such that it will only see the fly, not the nylon.

Reservoir boat tactics

It's not often that the larger waters stocked only with fry will have boats available but occasionally the local angling association may have their own which is available for hire. Catching specimens from these waters is a matter of relative sizes – there are going to be a lot of little chaps to every two-pounder. Apart from periods when larger terrestrials can bring the better fish to the top, you will rarely see

them rise and therefore subsurface tactics to avoid the small fish need to be carefully thought out. Lures are rarely effective and the fish will have got well accustomed to seeing groups of three flies twitching through the water. This standard wet fly approach is an excellent way of accumulating numerically large bags of fish but it means that most of the trout get caught at least once in their early life to these tactics and are therefore not likely to make the same mistake again as they grow older. You need to pursue a similar selective approach as when fishing the small clearwaters where stalking is not possible and use imitative patterns of say Damsel Nymphs or a Cove Pheasant Tail. Once again it's essential to fish these flies very slowly and to avoid striking at little plucks. Wait for a determined pull. I usually find that when a good fish decides to take the fly it will do so very positively. There's no halfway measures – it seems to be either complete indifference or a solid pull.

Casting presentation must be good as these waters are almost always very clear and the fish easily spooked. You'll need a leader of at least 15 ft and taper down to a single fly on a 4 lb point. Make use of a side wind if possible by allowing the ripple to drift the fly round with a minimum of retrieve to avoid line wake. Don't be misled by the relatively small size of these fish. They really can go and will pull line off a 6 or 7 outfit with no problem.

Bad weather conditions

On the exposed waters a good blow with overcast skies can often mean pretty poor general sport but an excellent chance of finding a big fish. Some of my best moorland reservoir trout have come under these conditions but you must be capable of controlling a line and boat in rough water as that's where the fish will be found. I think the bigger ones move out of their regular lies at these times and patrol the rough water of the shallows looking for easy pickings. A small Hopper pattern or a simple Damsel or Pheasant Tail cast across the waves and brought

back steadily is all that's needed. The fish will often be right at the very edge of the water in the real shallows.

Rises to terrestrials

Probably the easiest time of all to select a good trout from the upland reservoirs. There are very few specimen trout that will turn down the chance of easy pickings and a fall of hawthorne, ants, daddies or the like will mean having to scan large areas in order to spot every rise and assess its size. A very slow drift with one or sometimes two drogues will be needed and if you cast with a suitable dry fly at target fish it should result in a memorable day. A dry Wickhams or Sedge pattern are all that's needed for this style.

Reservoirs holding a good head

Punching out a long line at Farmoor. It's not easy sorting out the specimens on a concrete bowl but careful observation and interpretation of the rise forms can produce the goods.

of overwintered rainbows are of special interest to me and over the past ten years I have developed techniques to suit the two basic types by initially putting in a lot of time at Queen Mother Reservoir and then moving on to Bewl Water in Kent.

Boats on concrete bowl waters

Location of the fish on these waters is very much influenced by wind direction and ideally it needs to have been blowing from the same quarter for at least a few days. The windward shore line is usually the most productive area with other hotspots being in the lee of towers or piers close to the bank along which the wind is blowing. Some waters of irregular shape will develop unusual back currents which can surface on the edges of the sheltered bank in comparatively calm conditions and create an area of feeding activity which is difficult to recognize unless you know the water well. Early and late season are essentially times to make use of large lures or tandems to attract fry-feeding trout and, because I have never been too keen on the use of lead line tactics, I have worked out how to catch the big fish on slow-sinking lines to get plenty of sport from them. Where there is no bankside disturbance the trout will often be very close to the edge and an unleaded fly cast into the margins and allowed to slowly return along the bottom will interest them more than one which stays high in the water. A line weight corresponding to a Wet Cell II will, if slowly retrieved on the figure of eight style, keep a fly working ever deeper along the contour of the bank until it starts to lift up off the bottom towards the boat. This is a critical stage of the retrieve and trout following a fly will sometimes hit it very hard as it suddenly lifts

away from the bottom. I like to moor the boat on the 30-yard mark and can then cast into the bank but more importantly, parallel to it. Covering the strip of water at the bottom of the concrete slope and retrieving parallel to the shore with a simple lure on a very slow retrieve has brought me some super trout.

The slow, quiet approach is vital in all aspects of hunting big trout, particularly when at anchor. Fast stripping will involve a lot of additional casting and associated disturbance. While it is quite possible for a fish to move into the area around the boat you can't really expect resident fish to remain on the feed when flies are constantly being whipped through the water. By all means vary the rate of retrieve by putting in a few fast ones every so often, and if that proves to be the only way to get a take then you will get a better response by fan casting all around the boat rather than achieving saturation coverage by casting down the same line all the time. In addition, you will need to be constantly on the move when using fast retrieve tactics, and I can only say that my slow methodical approach has proved its worth many times.

Evenings on concrete bowls

This is the time when tradition maintains that the bigger fish lose their caution. While it's true that the onset of darkness must help to give them confidence, the weather conditions must also be correct. Evenings which suddenly become cold in the last hour or so of light are normally quite useless for fishing in the top layers and it's then that I concentrate on using a simple black tandem on something like a Hi-D shooting head. Fish the lure really slowly along the bottom in about 15 ft of water and most takes will come as the fly lifts off the bottom. In the last few minutes before the boats have to be in

there is often the best chance of all to connect with a large brownie. You need an area of completely undisturbed bank, a very quiet approach and delicate casts right into the very edge. Use an intermediate line, long leader and a small white lure. A hooked brown nearly always heads straight out into deep water and I have known them come right at the boat so that you cannot keep pace with the fish and prevent it fouling the anchor rope. Actually this is the one big danger with playing a large trout from a boat. I will never forget the look of utter dismay on the face of my friend Mike Dunstan when he lost a rainbow of at least 8 lb on Queen Mother Reservoir after it snagged the anchor rope in the closing stages of a long battle. The best thing you can do with a very large reservoir trout when fishing from an anchored boat is to let it run every time it heads away from the boat. If it wants to dive under the boat or kite around towards the anchor rope put the rod into the water as fast as possible and give it as much side strain as you dare away from the danger area. If you have a boat partner and the hooked fish is exceptional then retrieve anchor quickly.

Rough-weather days

A strong blow on a concrete bowl can produce a most interesting day if you have the nerve or authority to be out in a boat. Anchoring isn't easy but slowly dragging won't matter too much if you can do this parallel to a shore. Use a large white tandem on a 10 ft leader with a WF9 Fast Sinking Line and cast into the shore. Figure-of-eight retrieve and be prepared for the most delightfully positive takes. Late in the year seems to be the best period for these tactics and it doesn't matter if there are overnight frosts, although the taking period is then normally truncated into the 11.30–3 p.m. session.

Above
Nothing special by Farmoor standards but in a flat calm and bright sun every take is a bonus.

Left
An overwintered rainbow approaches the net on a misty day at Bewl Water when the trout were rising all around the boat for hours on end. It was a case of waiting and watching for the right fish to show itself.

Opposite
Bewl battlers of 6 lb 13 oz and 5 lb. Hook rainbows like these have grown-on in the reservoir and you'll ignore the tearaway stockies.

Opportunist days on concrete bowls

As you might expect, there are occasions when heavy hatches of fly such as buzzer or sedge bring bigger fish up to the surface where they can be tackled as individuals. A Cove Pheasant Tail cast to fish on buzzer and retrieved fast will kill very well. Similarly, falls of terrestrials like ants or daddies can provoke the same response.

Shoaling of fry at the back end of the season is also a most productive time for the larger trout and plastazote bodied patterns will invariably induce an offer. There is another technique with plastazote

Just what the boat angler wants – a sustained ripple and rainbows moving to the dry fly.

fry imitations which consistently picks up above average fish and that is to fish the fly on a two-foot leader attached to a lead core line. Let it all settle on the bottom in from ten to 30 ft of water and pull it in a foot at a time with long pauses. The trout will frequently take this fly well back in its throat.

Boat fishing on conventional reservoirs

Although my basic approach has been developed at Bewl Water in Kent, it can be applied to all our modern reservoirs where stock fish overwinter to produce the superbly conditioned grown-on specimens. I much prefer to concentrate on a single water rather

than flitting from one to another but occasional trips to such legendary waters as Blagdon and Rutland have proved that where this type of specimen occurs my methods work.

Finding the fish
I have already discussed obvious holding areas for big trout on reservoirs, but there are other ways of finding the specimens out in open water. I prefer to catch fish off the top and rarely resort to very fast sinking shooting heads unless the following conditions prevail.

Bright sun and calm, or wind and rain
These two very varied types of weather don't seem to be conducive to finding the better trout on the top. In these conditions, I rely on getting well anchored over a known deep drop off, old stream bed or off a promontory with at least 20 ft of water under the boat. I

then attach a big tandem and throw as long a line as possible, letting it sink well down in the water before starting a steady figure-of-eight retrieve, hoping to get the all-important take as the big fly starts its ascent to the boat. The very bright days are a time for using Polaroids to look down into the water to spot the fly and hopefully a following fish which can be induced to take much as you would on a small clear water fishery. The use of the very big fly and slow retrieve seems to sort through the basic-sized fish.

Lead core tactics
These very heavy lines demand the use of powerful rods and leaders around 10 lb breaking strain, and are very successfully used at anchor to present large flies in very deep water, particularly for specimen browns. It can be a very boring style of fishing but the rewards are sometimes

fantastic if you badly want a specimen brown. The more commonly used lead lining tactics are side casting from a drifting boat or just letting it all trail out behind. Although fish location and feeding depth can be difficult to predict, vast areas of water can be covered. The actual fishing demands very little in the way of skill but is nevertheless a ruthlessly efficient way of cropping growing-on stocks of brown trout.

Excessive use of these tactics once reduced Grafham's stocks of specimen browns to a trickle but they are now back again after a few years of everyone concentrating on Rutland. The effect here seems to be more marked as the stocking of browns has not led to a sufficiently high level of growing-on fish to allow such heavy cropping to continue without its eventual cleaning-up effect on the specimen trout stocks.

Fishing the upper layers

Much of what I have already said on catching specimens from naturally stocked reservoirs and from concrete bowls can also be applied to conventional reservoirs. Summarized, this is to capitalize on periods when the fish are up and showing, as a result of hatches of water-based fly or falls of terrestrials, allowing target fish to be located among the many ordinary ones. When conditions are right and fish are feeding off the top there are often days when you can only spot the very occasional specimen – and then only in one-off rises – so it's almost impossible to go for an observed individual. Rather surprisingly, I found that it works most effectively to fish a large Sedge pattern, or a Daddy later in the year, over areas of water about 20 ft deep where no other fish activity can be seen. Once again it's a method requiring great patience but a fly cast out and left for anything up to 15 minutes will often bring up a very

large trout. Quite why this should be so I just don't know. If ordinary-sized fish begin to show in the area you are covering then move on. The bigger fish just don't seem to swim with them at these times.

Most fly fishers want to be constantly casting and retrieving but you must develop the ability to sit and observe without fishing. I don't mind admitting that when using fly on or in the surface I very often don't strike if I can see that it's an unwanted smaller fish. This sometimes means ending the day without a 'limit bag' but I'm much happier with one fish over 3 lb than six at 1½ lb.

Evening tactics

Again this is often the most likely time of all to pick up a big trout and if I can't locate any risers among the also-rans then I use a small Black or White Lure on an intermediate and fish it about three feet down with a slow figure-of-eight retrieve. This will inevitably pick up the smaller fish as well but much less frequently than stripping tactics. And if you do hook a stockie it will often come off if given plenty of slack line. Quite why a big grown-on fish should take a simple lure at this stage of the day, when it must have seen similar efforts many times, is still a puzzle. But they do, and usually with a very convincing thump. A large standard Pheasant Tail is better in the high summer period.

Late season

When summer's extensive weed-beds are beginning to die back it's a time for quietly cruising along the reservoir edges and placing a dry fly about a foot from the weed in a simple searching session. Don't strike if a little fish flashes up but one of those old crafty lads that has spent the summer growing fat in the weeds will quite possibly roll over the fly in a way that instantly sets the adrenalin going. This, too, is the time for the big fry

feeders, and floating patterns off the edges of weed can be quite deadly.

Loch style

I'll reinforce my previous comments on this technique by saying that I don't feel it's at all selective for the bigger grown-on trout. True, it can be great fun to take fish like this but these are pot luck tactics – not what this book is about. Loch style primarily involves the use of three flies on a single leader but you will have noted that, yet again in this reservoir tactics section I advocate a single fly. After all you are only after one fish. Go for fish singly, don't confuse the issue by trying to cover your options with droppers.

Bank fishing

Reservoir banks can be a very hostile environment to the fisherman. Facing him is a vast expanse of water upon which even a 30-yard cast will not register: surely the big fish are all out in deep water? Not so; to grow large a trout must feed and the richest feeding is nearly always in the shallows around the banks. Dam walls can be likened to the sides of concrete bowls. They provide a growing medium for weed and algae on which snail and insect larvae can thrive – a ready-made larder with little escape, plus the sanctuary of deep water nearby if the fish senses danger. No wonder then that many very large trout are taken from such seemingly inhospitable areas. You won't often be able to capitalize on a good rise from such features but careful searching with a slow sink line and a leaded Hopper or nymph pattern fished slowly really can find those better trout.

Favourite days are when a strong, not a biting cold, wind is blowing right onto the dam or into one bank of a concrete bowl. You

Left
A slow drift on Hook Straight at Bewl with enough time to attempt interceptions of solid fish splashing at sedges.

Opposite
The exciting closing minutes when you know those wily reservoir monsters are on the prowl from their daytime hiding places under rearing cages. Maybe one last cast with a white lure . . .

Below
Fresh from the clear waters of Bewl Reservoir and perfectly hooked in the scissors.

will need good line control but a large fly fished on say a 6–9 ft leader will find the bigger fish which take full advantage of the rough conditions disturbing their favourite foods. Days like this will often bring long periods of non activity when it's easy to lose concentration constantly battling against the wind. Then comes an unexpected heavy pull and the leader is broken. I can remember many times on a variety of waters when numbed hands and brain just did not react properly.

Erosion

Wave action on conventional reservoirs gradually wears away the margins and produces extensive areas of shallows where insect life can thrive. When the bigger fish frequent these shallows you are up against the problems of presentation. A bungled cast can so easily spook the fish. You need to do all you can to avoid frightening off the trout and as these areas are best fished with imitative patterns you will need very long leaders, at least 20 ft, a single fly and very slow retrieves. The less often you can cast the better and a methodical search of an area of water can often best be achieved by using intermediate or slow-sink lines.

Bank tactics

All of the boat techniques such as observation, selection of target fish, and opportunist tactics are also very relevant to fishing from the bank but tackle needs to be more carefully considered. The ability to cast efficiently for a considerable distance is a prerequisite and aids to assist this are essential. The use of shooting heads or the double haul technique for weight-forward lines will give the necessary range of casts but other factors influence this ability. A line tray for wading to keep the line close to the angler and stop it sinking is an absolute must but it's so important to leave

the first few feet of line outside the tray when making the retrieve. You will also find that a slow retrieve produces less tangles in the backing than a stripping style of retrieve. To be effective off the bank, casting style must be good. When wading you have far less height above the water surface and therefore the back cast must be made high. Also, when fishing off dams or the sides of concrete bowls the back cast needs to clear the concrete or the fly will either be flicked off or blunted. A few hours spent with an instructor and plenty of practice can be well worth the effort when actually out on the water.

Wind

This is the biggest single deciding factor influencing the bank fisherman's choice of venue. Very strong winds blowing into the shallows can stir up the sediment so much that it's quite useless to fish, but the same wind blowing onto a more solid shoreline can give really excellent conditions. It very much depends on your casting ability to cope with strong winds but you can increase the odds of success by reducing leader length to some 6–8 ft, using braided leaders, a size heavier line than normal and careful positioning to use the wind off the left shoulder to increase casting range. Much is said about the thermocline layer which tilts subject to wind pressure but in my experience such bold stratification of water layers does not occur frequently enough to indicate where to fish on a large water. I quite agree that when the wind is blowing off a bank, then the fish can often be difficult to catch in that area but when the same wind blows terrestrials on to the water the fish soon find them and it's then a favourite spot for the angler. True – the majority of anglers use a back wind to help mediate inadequate casting abilities and as I

have already said the wind blowing on to a shoreline is where you will find fish feeding. Reservoir format with promontories, deeps, wooded banks, etc all have their effect on how the water behaves and where the fish will be. It's easy to give a stylized diagram of where to find the fish under certain ideal conditions but that type of day rarely occurs and I would recommend that you approach each outing with a completely open mind. By all means draw on past experience and that of other anglers on the water but remember you are looking for a minority of the reservoir's stock, therefore plan accordingly. If there are no obvious clues to help locate feeding trout then go for recognized holding areas near deep water. Some days you just won't get any response at all from the bigger trout and I'm personally more than happy to then use the trip to gain experience on the basic fish.

Fishing reservoirs from the bank in search of specimens can be a bit soul destroying unless conditions are favourable and I honestly don't think it's worth slogging away during the main part of the day unless it is overcast and rough or there is a specific feeding activity going on. Far better to use the time in observation of likely areas or just watching along the edges of weed beds for signs of a large fish. Fry time at the back end of the season is a classic for this and a couple of hours spent in locating and observing the feeding habits of a big trout are worth all the effort. Continued search-style casting may well produce a big fish just by chance – but blind luck is no substitute for skill. You won't get a specimen trout every day but make use of all the tactics and locating advice I have given and there's no reason why you should not then achieve the capture of some memorable fish. TIGHT LINES!

RECOGNISED WATERS FOR SPECIMEN TROUT

Small waters
Clear water – stalking tactics
Avington Trout Fishery, Nr. Winchester, Hants.
Three lakes totalling 13 acres (5.25 hectares)
0962 78312

Chalk Springs Fishery, Arundel, Sussex.
Two lakes totalling 4 acres (1.6 hectares)
0903 883742

Damerham Fisheries, Fordingbridge, Hants.
Six lakes.
072 53 446

Dever Springs, Andover, Hants.
Two lakes.
0264 72592

Nythe Lake, Alresford, Hants.
096 273 2776

Rockbourne Trout Fishery, Sandelheath, Fordingbridge, Hants.
Six lakes totalling 8 acres (3.2 hectares)
072 53603

Rooksbury Mill, Andover, Hants.
Two lakes 3 and 7 acres (1.2 and 2.8 hectares)
0264 52921

Clear water – searching tactics
Church Hill Farm, Mursley, Bucks.
Two lakes, 10 acres (4 hectares)
029 672 524

Ringstead Grange, Kettering, Northants.
0933 622960

Vicarage Spinney Trout Fishery, Milton Keynes, Bucks.
02806 363

Willow Pool, Eynsham, Oxford.
0865 882215

Coloured water
Aveley Lakes, Aveley, Essex.
5 acres (2 hectares)
0926 613344

Bayham Lake Trout Fishery, Kent.
16 acres (6.5 hectares)
0892 890276

Stafford Moor Fishery, Dolton, Devon.
Two lakes, 20 acres (8 hectares)
080 54 360

Willinghurst Trout Fishery, Shamley Green, Surrey.
5 lakes, 10 acres (4 hectares)
0483 275048

Naturally stocked reservoirs
Colliford Reservoir, Bodmin, Cornwall.
0579 42366
Crowdy Reservoir, Camelford, Cornwall.
0579 42366
Stithians Reservoir, Redruth, Cornwall.
0326 72544

Wales, Yorkshire, the Lake District and Scotland offer many waters containing natural stock with plenty of opportunities to search for specimens.

Conventionally stocked reservoirs
Bewl Water, Lamberhurst, Kent
0892 890352
Blagdon, Nr. Bristol
0761 62577
Chew, Nr. Bristol
0272 332339
Draycote Reservoir, Rugby, Warks.
0788 811107
Farmoor II Reservoir, Oxford
0865 863033
Grafham Water, Bedfordshire
0480 810247
Ladybower, Nr. Sheffield
0433 51424
Pitsford Water, Northants
0604 781350
Queen Mother Reservoir, Datchet, Berks.
0753 683605
Rutland Water, Leicestershire
078 086 770

RECORDING THE CATCH

Besides the importance of keeping a written record of all your fishing expeditions with details of the fish caught, it is also very satisfying to have really good photographs or indeed a permanently mounted trophy. Most fishing photographs tend to be of unsightly lumps scattered on the bank or of a headless angler trying to show off a good fish with its body obscured by hands. It's possible to do a lot better than this. I carry with me a 35mm compact camera loaded with colour slide film, since magazines can print pictures from a good quality slide easier than from a print. Character shots of fish being played or netted are always interesting and its as well to remember that a fish soon loses its colour when killed so get the shots done quickly. With a good specimen there is a little trick to use if you want to have top quality photo-graphs taken later in the day or indeed the following day. Look after the fish by keeping it cool, preferably lying in cold water out of the sun. Before you want to photograph it lay the fish flat, clean it off and cover the show side in Cling Film. Leave it for half an hour and the colours will come back. It works as well if the fish is left in a fridge or the top of a freezer. My record trout was photographed looking as if it had just come out of the water, five hours after capture and some forty miles away by using this technique. When you hold a specimen trout try to wear bright coloured clothing such as a red or blue shirt so the fish stands out and keep the fish up by your chest not down below the waist, holding it with one hand in the gill plate and a finger of the other hand in its vent so as to display the body properly. Pull the fish apart slightly to avoid belly sag and you should then get a good shot.

Following on from a quality photograph is the ultimate momento of having the fish mounted. Here there are a number of options available from the traditional bow fronted glass cased mount to the fish mounted on a board more as a trophy. It all depends on the skills of the taxidermist in shaping the body and fins before restoring the original colours with paint. There are some awful mountings around: remember you generally get what you pay for. Look at examples of work before committing your fish. A good taxidermist won't get the fish back to you for at least nine months so you can save up the cash in that time. I fully recommend having your fish mounted, it not only always reminds you of the catch, but is a very decorative feature in a house and constantly provokes conversation.

GLOSSARY

A.F.T.M. Abbreviation for Association of Fishing Tackle Manufacturers. Set standards for line weights, ranging upwards from No. 1 Rods, lines and reels are all rated to these standards.

Beaching Technique whereby a fish is drawn on its side into shallow water, maintaining a tight line with the fishes struggles pushing it out of the water.

Buzzer larval stage of chivenomids.

Clear waters Where visibility into the water may be as much as 20' deep if light angles are correct.

Coloured waters Where it is impossible to look into the water due to either algal growth or suspended particulate matter.

Concrete bowl Man made reservoir with concrete sides generally raised above surrounding landscape.

Dog Nobbler Registered name for type of lure using long tail of marabou fibres.

Double haul Technique to increase line speed for distance casting.

Drogue Square sheet of canvas type material with a hole in middle. Tied at each corner it acts as a sea anchor to slow a drifting boat.

Droppers Short length of nylon protruding from main leader for fishing more than one fly at a time.

Dry Fly An artificial fly which floats on or in the surface film.

Ethafoam Type of plastic foam used to line fly boxes or construct floating fry patterns. It does not absorb water.

Extension butt Short section of handle to fit into end of rod to give extra leverage.

Fingerling Immature trout of some 3 to 5 inches long.

Grown-on Term for trout which have evaded capture and continue to grow from one year to the next after stocking.

Hardy Renowned tackle company based at Alnwick, Northumberland.

Lamiglass American manufacturer of rods and blanks.

Lead core Fly line with central core of lead for very deep fishing.

Leader Length of nylon between fly and fly line.

Line tray Device to retain backing for long distance casting.

Lure A 'fly' which does not resemble any aquatic life form.

Nymph Larval stage of insect development or type of fly.

Sedge Common term for adult trichoptera insect characterised by 'roof' shape of wings when at rest.

Stewpond Concrete or earth pond or net cage in which fish are grown by feeding with pellets.

Stringer Simple length of cord or more specialised device to suspend the catch in water to keep it fresh.

Tandems System of mounting hooks to produce a large lure.

Terrestrials Insects whose habitat is dry land but which may get blown or fall onto water at a particular stage of their life cycle.

Wet cell Trade name for sinking line.

Wet fly Common term for the 'traditional' flies fished just under the surface.

Wind lane A distinct flatter area in the rippled surface of a reservoir. Varies in width and can be several hundred yards long.

INDEX

Page numbers in *italic* refer to illustrations